Manual of Personal Prophetic Prayer

© Copyright Sheri Hauser 2020
© Copyright for art by Karna Peck, KPO
Published by Glorybound Publishing
SAN 256-4564
10 9 8 7 6 5 4 3 2 1
Printed in the United States of America
KDP ISBN 9781076761583
Copyright data is available on file.
Hauser, Sheri, 1957-
    Manual of Personal Prophetic Prayer/Sheri Hauser
    Includes biographical reference.
1. Prophecy   2. Prayer   3. Charismatic
I. Title

www.gloryboundpublishing.com
www.karnapeck.com

The painting used for the cover of Foundational Prophetic Prayer is from the gallery of Karna Peck. It is entitled Hole in Heaven. Prints may be ordered from Glorybound Publishing. More of her art may be seen on *www.karnapeck.com.*

Sheri's Dream Books

12 Steps in the Garden

Coriantá
Tomaseña
Katísha
Míracules
Pillow Talk
Sinactía Empezía
Camezía Reptídad
Kapaseus
Festevía
Firefly
Seedlings
Wedding Service

More Dream Books

Abreas Ansus
Adoration and Reverence
Aurora Dream Journal
Chalísha
Coriantá Love Notes 1-10
Dove Dreams Fly
Dreamatrix Emmanuel
Flowing Down River
Holy Hum
Interpretation of Art
Manual of Church Prophetic Prayer
Manual of Personal Prophetic Prayer
Me Mesa
Palagra
Palazzo Lascett
Reflections of Praise
Religion

Healing Prayers Booklets

Battle of Nun booklet
Fast Track Healing booklet
Hope for Tomorrow booklet
Preparing for Eternity booklet
Repentance for Yesterday booklet
Strength for Today booklet
Vacuum Cleaner Salesman booklet

Dream Cachë

Welcome to Sheri's dream cache releasing what has been kept hidden until now. There are stores of riches kept in a vault up to this day, which open the door of understanding the voice of God in dreams as answers to prayer. The wind, the storm, the rain and the lightening of God is coming. Feel the wind? There is always a gentle breeze just before the tornado. Oh how we have looked for the eye of the storm in this world in which we live, yet we have not found it. We have prayed, yet we are not healed. We have spent countless hours on our knees without finding our deliverance. Our children remain on drugs; our families are still in bondage; we are yet poor and destitute. Our Churches are poor, filled with empty pews and singers off cue. Where are the answers to our prayers? We have been tricked by our enemies. They have snuck in and left seeds of doubt which grew into a cancer eating away at our faith in God. Our vision has been clouded by our own sinfulness and lust for the things of this world. Yet we continue to seek for a force outside ©ourselves which will save us from this dreadful condition which we are in. Where is He? Take encouragement, friends, I have brought a fresh shipment of hope: It's the hope of hearing the voice of God for yourself. Just like Moses heard the voice of the Lord and brought Salvation to the Children of Israel, He is bringing the same today. Has God changed? No. Suppose you ask a question in prayer: Do you expect an answer? There is one, you know? I am here to help you reach out to God in a special way and enable the enemies of doubt within your life to be crushed and conquered. What I bring is a bridge to faith. We attempt to reach a God we do not know; only have heard about from those going on before us. But, when we reach into that darkness, we are unsure of a connection: Will there be a hand reaching back to us? We don't really know. That is faith, my friend. Faith reaches into the unknown seeking something you are unsure of while trusting that there will be an answer on the other side. Welcome to my dream Cachë. It is like a jewelry box filled with gems, sparkling in the moonlight: dreams that come to life as the voice of God dances through my head night after night. And, He wants the same for you. He told me, so. Your dreams and visions can be a bridge to a relationship with God giving encouragement, hope, help, and direction hidden in this vault of

wondrous pictures
sent straight
from
heaven.
I have propped open
for you five doors
and a window.
I encourage
you to

learn to seek God through learning to understand His voice as it comes to you His way, now as you are comfortable accepting it. Remember, God came in thunder, storm and a wind in times before. Why wouldn't He now? May I present this shipment of Grace. For it is by the Grace of God that we are saved. Remember that.

MANUAL OF
PERSONAL PROPHETIC PRAYER

Private Prophetic Prayer

By
Sheri Hauser

Glorybound Publishing
Camp Verde, Arizona
2020

Letter from the Author

It took 12 years to compile the 12 Steps in the Garden to Intimacy with God. Just as I was completing the final book, Seedlings, I had a dream and God informed me there were two more books imbedded in my old files. I as very surprised, and began combing my acres of files stuffed with dreams and messages from God which I carefully wrote down over several years. In my amazement, I found two subjects which were complete with outlines and pieces carefully laid out!

One 'book' is Reflections of Praise. This is poetry. The other is on the subject of prophetic prayer. By way of background, I led the prayer team at Church for several years earnestly seeking to meet God with our requests at the same place of His desire. It became a testing ground for prophetic prayer. We met, as a small group a couple of hours before Church and knelt on the floor crying on the altar for the needs of the congregation. A glory circle developed and often we became 'sunburned' during these prayer times. Such a bond was developed as we poured out our hearts and allowed the Spirit of God to move through us entreating for the hearts of others. Most of these individuals are still on my speed dial. I call them and we meet for intense prayer; prophetic prayer.

Prayer is the only time when we pray the request, walk toward the answer and it comes to meet us. Miracles happen. Souls are saved and people are healed.

There is an intersection of prayer like two lines meeting at a specific intersection. We pray and God answers. We rush toward the place; and in a split second, He rushes toward us with the answer. There is nothing to compare with asking for something which is God's desire...because it is sure to occur. That is Prophetic Prayer.

Sections

Spiritual Prayer
Benefits of Prophetic Prayer
Prophetic Gifts
Using the Gifts as Tools to Pray
Cafea

Index of Writings

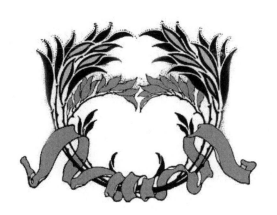

What is prophetic Prayer?
Prophecy defined

In Heaven a Door Stands Open

God has given us the keys to the Kingdom of Heaven. He has given us the ability to pray with faith that removes mountains. When we see where we are going, we will have faith to be sure that is where we will end up. Often, we see situations as a huge pile of rocks in our way.

It is time to put on our bathing suits and go into the sea. The Sea of Knowledge, wisdom and revelation that God longs to surround us with. He will open our eyes to see the real mountains. These are not the visible ones, but the invisible ones; the spiritual mountains put there by the sea monster, Leviathan.

Often, when we swim, the water feels cold. Our emotions may be cold to what God wants us to do. We can't tell the seasons of God by feeling. Our emotions will not tell us what to do. We have to know in our heart and believe the Word of God.

He wants to remove the mountains from our life. He has given us the authority to cast them a new role in our lives. The mountain melts when our spiritual eyes are opened to see the desires of the Kingdom of God in the situation. When we see them, we will become aware of them. We cannot deal with something that we cannot see. They are as piles of rocks placed there by the enemy. These are mountains of guilt, oppression, doubt, anxiety, dread, sickness, loneliness, etc. We should cast them out like Jesus cast demons out of those who were oppressed. God has already given us the authority as children of God, to deal with them through the blood of Jesus Christ.

Exodus 15:22, Deuteronomy 2.1, Job 38.8, Psalms 46.2-4, 48,98.7, 52.7,124.4, Isaiah 10.26-27, 11.9-15, 27.1, 33.21 Song of Solomon 4.15, Jeremiah 5.22, Zechariah 9.4, Matthew 4.18, 8.27,21.21, Mark 1.16, John 21.7, I Corinthians 10.2, Revelation 4.6, 15.2.

Spiritual Domination

Many times we think that it is our soul, our will that dominates our moral character. But this is not true. When we are born again, the Holy Spirit takes up residence in our spirit. This Holy Spirit writes His laws on our hearts. He etches His character on us; His character of Holiness. (Proverbs 16:18, Hoses 4:12). His Spirit within us provides the source of one's insight. It is the Holy Spirit within that etches the impressions on the mind and then helps to interpret them to bring them to the paper.(I Corinthians 2:11)

When we become children of God through belief in Jesus Christ as our Savior, we become sensitive to inner voice of Holy Spirit. We receive a spirit of adoption as sons by which we cry out "Abba! Father!" (Romans 8:15). This new adoption enables us to think spiritually dominated by God. The Spirit Himself (God's Holy Spirit) testifies with our spirit that we are children of God (Romans 8:16). The same new spirit gives mind of Christ to believer (I Corinthians 2:16). You are renewed in the spirit of your mind when you have the new spirit. When we focus on God, then He will to talk into your mind. He will etch the 'word of God' on your painting. Hebrews 10:16 says, "This is the covenant that I will make with them: After those days, says the Lord: I will put My laws upon their heart, and on their mind I will write them."

When we become Christians, then we are to serve in the midst of the others. We come as an empty vessel, a cup, and He fills us up with whatever He sees will bring us the ultimate happiness. We hold in our hands whatever we are supposed to give to others on behalf of Him. We display His love to the world through the use of our gifts when we offer praise to Him for them. We are not responsible for the results, only to give the cup; to give of ourselves. We must leave the results of our ministry in the hands of the master artist, God.

Why does He Give us the Message?

Our primary purpose is to utilize our talents to praise Him. We have been entrusted with gifts which we are supposed to develop for the use of the Church body. When we become complacent in the use of them, there is a curse of God that will bring withered hands and blindness. Obedience to use the gifts God has entrusted us with allows us to become slaves to righteousness which leads to Holiness. Sharing our gifts with others brings unification of the body of Christ and permits others to enter into our acceptable sacrifice of Praise.

Many times others do not see our 'talent'. We may become discouraged. But , we must remember that we are living in a time that the enemy is fighting hard against us. He knows that he has only a short time and he will be chained in Hell forever. Even though, as loyal servants of Christ, we are spread out, do not be discouraged. He has called us and He will multiply us because of His righteousness. We are supposed to bring everything into the house of God, so the temple can be built. God needs every tool for the Kingdom of God to be built. Just because others may say that your art is bad, in God's eyes it is an essential tool that he needs to display his character and teaching. We are the display of God's righteousness to the world through our gifts in unity with our relationship in Christ Jesus. As children of God, he calls us stars in his Kingdom. He wants us to shine for Him. Just like comets, we are in motion and each display a tail of a different color. No two stars are alike. We all shine for him, but display different characteristics within his Kingdom. There may be many with similar gifts, but each has a wonderful tail of a different color.

Stranded on the Rooftop

I stand on the rooftop and call out to you.
Is there anyone out there?
I scream with all my breath, to hear only my echo return.
Is there anyone out there?
My home has been destroyed, my life a scorn
I am left all alone, simply to die and morn.
Where is did my help go, I wish I knew?
How can I survive without life anew?
For, my life is at risk and my family all apart.
There seems no one to listen to my crying heart.
Is there any one out there?
From the flood of my thoughts, my possessions are afloat.
I sit here on the roof looking at all the writ I wrote.
For all is lost and nothing is to be had
If my life is all alone. Certainly that would be bad.
Is there anyone out there?
For, day after day, year after year I call out to you
A God who happens to be your Father all the way through
And you thought I wasn't listening, how do you think I feel?
For, I have been stranded aloft, left to fish without a reel.
I have called out day and night, running through your mind
And again and again, I have been someone you could not find.
Is there anyone out there?
How my voice burns for a response to my plea
To hear from my family would make my heart glad with glee.
Yet, I paint signs in the sky and dip my brush to color the clouds.
I write day and night, yet your mind remains in shrouds.
Come to My house, and rescue my lonely heart.
Be my deliverer, bring your part.
For, this heart is separated by the gap you refuse to cross.
It's a line in the sand that has become dental floss.
Stuck in your teeth, becoming a grind,
This gap of sin only I can un wind.

Empty Plate

A gift is a present given by God. The gifts that he has given to his body are for feeding his sheep. He feeds them with the characteristics of himself. We are to bring an empty plate to the table. We go the table hungry, not full.

Are we eating ahead of time? What do I feed on?

An empty plate is one that can be etched on as plates that money is printed with . don't come with predisposed ideas of what God intends to do. We don't have any idea of what he wants to do in another's life. Don't plan ahead what to say. let god tell you then.

Words: *The gift is food for others. Bring an empty plate.*

Interpretation:

We need to put away our predisposed ideas of what God wants to do. We need to come to him with an open plate; be a plate that he can write on. He wants to write on our heart with his messages. The plate is like one that is used to print money.

Rolling out the Red Carpet for a Vision

It takes more than endurance to roll out the vision. A vision is like a welcome rug. You need to roll it out as it was rolled up; with the intentions God created it for, otherwise it will serve no purpose but to honor the enemy. There is no middle ground when it comes to the kingdom of God on earth; either we are on one side or the other. Unless we make a conscious decision to serve God or we default to the enemy's side.

To roll out the welcome runner, you need to become one. You have to run the race with desire, determination and speed keeping your eyes fixed on the goal; otherwise the rug will be rolled out in the wrong direction. Picture in your mind the way they roll out a red rug for a celebrity when he is arriving on a jet. There is expense, timing and preparation involved. The individual has to purchase the rug, get the proper papers in order to be able to do it, and be there to actually roll it out in the right place at the right time.

Imagine how good it feels to be at the right place with the right stuff at the right time? What if you didn't want to spend the time, money and effort to get it all ready? Will it affect the arrival of the intention of God? Yes. God can go where ever He wants with whomever He desires. He only works with willing hearts who desire to honor His plans and purposes. Why would he land at an airport who was not expecting Him? Why would he go to a place where there is no greeting party when there is an option to arrive at a destination where one is ready?

Do not be dissuaded into passivity regarding the coming of the vision. God keeps His word because He has the omnipotent power to do it.

Sheri, the difference with you, is that you didn't invest

in a rug; you invested in an airport. You went out to the desert and purchased a large lot of ground. Then, being high in debt, you just went into the center and sat on a rock. Surely, you reasoned, there will be a bolt of lightning which will strike and this place an instantly it will be as it should; an airport will rise out of the sand. You waited, and waited, and waited. Day turned into night and night into daytime. Yet, it was just you and your rock sitting all alone in the desert owned by another, yet holding you prisoner for payment.

And, the enemy mocked, "Where is your God, now? Has he deserted you? Who would send His daughter into the desert to purchase a property for an airport spending all of her years on an aimless project? Surely your God is dead."

Often I ignored the taunting, only to find some shred of truth which crawled up my leg to deliver a stinging bite. But, sometimes I entertained the argument and engaged the enemy in battle for territory. He was right; I didn't own it, I was a debtor to pay for an intention clearly given to me by God. Yes, I reasoned; but I am a legal debtor who has made a binding agreement to prepare for the vision to arrive. After the shock of being put into such an odd position wore off, I realized the rock was getting colder day by day as a chair, so I went back to God to see if there were a few things I could do before actually smoothing out the runway.

"Ah," He said, "I am so glad you have arrived into my courtyard, daughter. How is it going with the airport in the desert?"

"God, you see and know everything. This airport thing isn't working out so well. My husband hates me for running us into debt and wants to have me committed for hearing voices and writing books; my friends think I am weird; and this vision has many desiring to come aboard the vision before it starts. They are impatient and rude.

I feel caught in the middle between Your desires and my inability to make it happen."

"Precisely said, Sheri. It takes a miracle to bring about the promises of God. Are you God? Did you tell them you are God? Did you promise that which you have no ability to fulfill?"

"No. I said, you said."

"And…they don't believe," God said.

"Yes. Because it has never been done, they don't think it is possible. And, because I have an unassuming presentation, they are not impressed into believing. I guess if I caused rain to fall by speaking or was able to strike someone with a lightning bolt, they would believe my words came from God and believe me."

"Funny girl! You already do. And, did they believe? Miracles have come by your hand over and over. They were impressed, but they cannot fathom the direct line you have with your heavenly father because they have no idea what it is about. Faith comes by the hearing the word of God. Their ears are full of wax and not open to My voice. What does it say…They will hear my voice and I will call to them. How can they come to Me if they do not know which way to walk? But, if they cannot hear My voice, then their steps are insanity walking in all directions without true purpose.

And, you come along telling them you hear my voice so clearly as to write it down word for word…and you think it odd they don't believe."

Well, it doesn't help to have people mocking you when you are trying to do something you think is from God.

I agree. But, you live in the world. That is the price for living in the world. You are surrounded by disbelief in things which are not of the world; things which are not tangible.

Sorry, I got off track feeling sorry for myself. Please

continue.

In order for a vision to come to pass it has to meet the provision, the purposes and the timing at exactly the right place.

Where do I come in?

I need a rug roller.

The difference between the voice and the person.

There is a difference between the voice of someone and him.

The voice is the sound that is made to form words when we put air behind it. That is exactly why some can't hear the voice of God. They have no air.

Didn't Jesus say, "I breathe on you and you will receive the Holy Spirit?"

In order for someone to breathe on you, you need to be close enough to feel it, but, we are too afraid to get that close.

Section 1

Benefits of Prophetic Prayer

God's Antenna

Word: *We need to be God's Antenna: To sit in his presence and display his love to others.*

He has provided guidance systems for us, but we need to turn on our radar system. Put up our antenna.

We need to tune our receiver to God's channel. He has a 24 hr network channel that he is televising over to us. When we sit in his presence, we get on his channel. We tune into what he is all about.

We receive Jesus Christ as our Lord and Savior when we ask him to cleanse us of our sins. He does it. But we must continue to receive him; to receive his word to us. It's like marrying someone then never speaking to them when we stop receiving him day after day. We are to become children of God and he wants to have a relationship with us; one of communication. He has given us the Spirit of Truth will guide us into all truth. The Holy Spirit he will speak only what he hears and he will tell us about God's Kingdom yet to come. His purpose in displaying this information to us is so that our joy may be made full.

There are no signals from God apart from him sending them to us. We cannot find him on our own. Our antennas aren't big enough to catch his signals. When we come to him on his standards and humbly accept the word that he longs to instill in us, it will save us from a lot of ills in our lives. God calls us to receive the word of God as it actually is, the word of God not as the word of men and allow it to work in us. The word of God is active and works in us to change our lives. When we have a dream and take the time to interpret it and work it into our lives the interpretation of the dream causes gifts and rewards and honor to us. Interpretation of dreams needs to be shown. The dream may be shown to us, but the interpretation needs to be shown to others for them to understand the Kingdom of God.

We are not without help in interpreting the messages that God longs to send us. He has sent the Holy Spirit into our hearts. Our hearts call out, "Abba, Father" We receive the full rights of sons. Though we haven't seen him, he will teach us how to love him. He will give us the ability to believe in him and be filled with a joy that can only be found through a relationship with him. As we ask things of him, he opens the doors of communication to us and answers us. He longs to share with us the knowledge of the secrets of the Kingdom of God. As obedient children, we are to listen to advice and accept his loving instruction.

There is an inheritance from God waiting for us as we walk into his words with obedience to them. He desires for us to lose the kingdom of this world and exchange it for the goals of the Kingdom of Heaven. This will provide us with true life and happiness. We will live with the power of the Holy Spirit. He will enable us to be faithful to the obedience of God's words to us. When we are faithful in a little, he will give us more

God has commissioned his Children with a message to others to open their eyes to turn them from darkness to light and from the power of Satan to Him that they may receive forgiveness of sins and a place among those who are sanctified by faith in Jesus. There is reconciliation to God through our Lord Jesus Christ.

We receive revelation, knowledge, prophecy and words of instruction from the Holy Spirit. The communion of God through Jesus Christ we are to pass on to others; the bread and the wine. Break off a piece of our bread for them so they can multiply it in their own lives. Give them some of a part of your delight in the Holy Spirit so that they can learn to delight in him as well. Whatever we have seen, received, or heard we are to put it into practice and display it to others. We need to be careful that nothing squelches out the word of God coming to us. The daily worries will try to choke out our time and thoughts. Pleasures will try to consume our time. Then there is the present adversary, the Devil who will fight us at every turn. But God has called us to preserver because when we have stood the test, we will receive the crown of life that God has promised to those who love him. The chief Shepherd will appear and we will receive a crown of Glory that will never fade away.

References
Proverbs 19:20, Daniel 2;6, Matthew 7.8, 10.8, Luke 8.13,9, John 1;.12-16,16.14-24, Romans 1.5, 5.11, I Corinthians 14.5, Hebrews 9.15, Philippians 4.9, Romans 15.7, Galatians 4.5, Colossians 3.24, The 2.10, James 1.21, 1 Peter 1.9, 5.4

Talking Bird of Prophecy

The Dream:
I am in a mud room of a house (ante-room where you remove your boots before entering the house). The door is open and a large beautiful black bird fly into the room. It is a tropical bird with shiny feathers and a crimson ring around its eye. It talks to me. It has flown in through the garage because the door is open. I follow the bird out into the garage. It takes the garage door opener and hides it up in the rafters out of my reach. Then it shows me some caged birds. As I look at the caged birds, I notice two green parrots who have only known captivity and two beautiful blue baby birds who have been caught and put into the cage. The blue birds are sad and look like they are about to die. They are walking amidst the droppings in the bottom of the cage. As I pick up the cage under the instruction of the black bird, there is no back to the cage at all. Once the cage is picked up, the birds could fly free. He tells me to let the blue birds go free and to place the parrots in with the puppies who are caged also in the garage. There are four puppies, as there were four birds. They are in a cage in the center of the garage. This cage does not have any walls, but the puppies are staying in.

Interpretation:

The black bird symbolizes God's Word carried through his messenger service on the wind (the Holy Spirit). It often comes through the darkness- the gift of dreams at night. The red circle around the eye gives special attention to the vision which is encircled by representation of the blood of Jesus. The blood of Jesus Christ encircles the vision of the Word for His people.

The messenger finds me in the ante-room with my

shoes removed as I realize that going into the dwelling place of God (the presence of His Holiness) requires cleansing. The bird is a tame bird that has been taught to say only what the master wants it to say. God's word to us comes as a collection of parables. "The words of the wise are like goads; collected sayings like firmly driven nails, given by one shepherd." He knows precisely what we need as a church and distributes to us as we need. Nothing will be missing because it all comes from One Shepherd. The Word will bring insight, prudence, knowledge, discretion, discerning, guidance.

God's vision for us is to be totally free as He takes the garage door opener and moves it out of the way. A garage is a place where things are stored for the 'next season'. As God has taken me to the garage, He makes me aware that the 'tools of God' need to be taken out at their seasons. We have stored them rather than listen and be aware of when God wants to use His tools in His Kingdom. He longs to build a Kingdom.

The caged birds are innocent truths that God has provided for His people. Rather than building a nest for them, they have put them in storage. The cage is of deception built by the enemy. Thinking we need to 'save things for a different season'.

The cage is a weaving of deceit by the enemy to which we are being held in captivity. Waywardness and complacency caused by our stubbornness and rebellious heart has caused us to turn from recognizing the sovereignty of God in our lives. We have permitted our Church to be taken captive by Satan (using the reproach of men as his weapon). We have listened to false prophecy because it has allowed us to be complacent. We trample the needy and do away with the poor. We haven't given to the true needs of the people. We have taught them to be religious. The true needs are companionship with God, nurturing by the Divine Shepherd. We need to release prayer and praise within the Church.

The birds are representative of prayer...the ones on the floor that are blue...and praise...the parrots that sing all the time, even when caged. I'm not sure why there are two of each. The puppies represent companionship with the master. We need to take it out of storage and bring it into the bedroom. The bird tells me to allow the parrots to join the puppies and to release the blue birds. Prayer would be released, and praise would become joined with companionship with Our Shepherd. All need to be taken out of the garage because it is the season.

The promises of God have been paraphrased by the leaders. It is deceit of humanism and flesh. They are for self-gain and spend more time placating each other than caring for the needs of the people. They do not give from a pure heart, but expect loyalty and following. They sell the sweepings with the wheat. Gossip and smut with the Word of the Lord. There is a famine of hearing the words of the Lord.

According to the principles of prophetic prayer I looked up several sections of scripture and prayed them. We will go into this process in the last chapter of the book on practicing prophetic prayer. I have included them in the introduction to give the reader a sense of the spirit of prophetic prayer. I feel it is extremely important to understand the interrelationship between the standard, which is the Bible, and prophetic words, visions and dreams (which are words for today). According to the teaching direction I received in the dream, I prayed the following sections of Scripture. Notice I pulled from Old Testament and New Testament portions. As I have notebooks full of these interactive prayer times, I will list several of them in the last section of the book to further give examples.

Verses Prayed

Ecc 10:20 A bird of the air may carry your words.
Jer 5:20 people with stubborn and rebellious heart
Jer 5:26 Wicked men set snares for birds.

v30 Prophets prophecy lies, priests rule by their own authority and my people love it this way. But what will you do in the end?

v 27 cages...trap woven of wicker/ deceit....a basket of deceit.

Amos 8   People are a basket of ripe fruit. Woven Deceit

v5 Buy the poor with silver and needy for sandals. Leaders only pause for religious activities, then cont. to lock up the poor. People are hungry, needy and poor... what they get is jail time. Leaders sell things God gives for free. Set themselves up as judges with dishonest scales. Tip the scale toward opinions of leaders and placation of those in spiritual authority rather than needs of the people. They paraphrase the Word of God with humanism and flesh. Do not give from pure heart. Sell the sweepings with the wheat. Sell smut with the Word.. resulting in a **famine of hearing the Words of God**.

Ez 7:23 Bound because of pride.

Jer 12:1-17 God's Justice. I will have compassion if they learn well the ways of my people and swear by my Name. They will be established.

Gen 7:14-15 Birds are creatures with the breath of life and wings.

Gen 15 Birds used as a sacrifice in covenant of Abraham with God. Fire passed between them.

Lev 14:1-7 Birds used in purification. Kill one bird and release the other. the released bird is dipped in the blood of the other bird with fresh water.

The bird smells death but it is freed. Together with

cedar wood, fresh water and scarlet yarn. Cedar speaks of sacrifice and scarlet yarn is the thread of Jesus' blood through time. Water is the Holy Spirit's cleansing.

Duet 14:11 Don't eat unclean birds.

Duet 22:6 God wants to ensure propagation of birds.

Job 41:5 Can't have Satan in a cage as a pet bird.

Ps 11 Can't run from the wicked. We are like birds. We have to seek protection from God.

Ps 104:1-35 God's birds are free. Next to the waters. sing amongst the branches. Different birds live in different places. God provided the food and the seasons.

v25 God provides season and food

v 28 God provides and the birds gather and build.

v30 God's Spirit causes renewal...Praise

Ps 124 The snare is broken when we call out to the Lord. Our help is in the 'name' of the Lord

Pr 6:1-5 we are trapped by our own words, enslaved by the words of our mouth. (We claim to meet needs instead of God for others.)

v5 free yourself by humbling yourself before your neighbor.

Prov 7 Snare...waywardness. It is being in the wrong place at the wrong time. Not noting the seasons and times. False prophecy is an adultress that causes waywardness.

Prov 26:2 Words are like a sparrow. They fly by if undeserved.

Ecc 9:12 Men are trapped by evil times: being somewhere at the wrong time.

Ecc 11:9-11

Ecc 12:1-14 Trusting in your own strength is a cage of deceit. Makes a listless bird. Causes: darkness, discouragement, decrease in numbers of people, closed doors, faint songs, fear of danger, loss of desire for life, mourning. If your life is based on life here on earth, it is as fragile as a bird.

v11 Wise words are like goads, the collected sayings like firmly embedded nails--given by one Shepherd. Loving reverence for God.

Isa 31:5 Like birds hovering overhead, the Lord will shield us. He passes over like he passed over the sin in Egypt and spared them to rescue them.

Lam 2 False visions of prophets do not reveal sin and ward off captivity.

v18 Let the hearts of the people arise and cry out to the Lord--O wall of the Daughter of Zion let your tears flow. Pour out your heart like water in the presence of the Lord...for the lives of your children who faint from hunger.

v 22 those I cared for the enemy has destroyed. Bitterness, hardship. They are walled in, weighted down, their prayer is shut out. The way is barred with blocks, the path crooked and we are left mangled without help. Our heart is pierced.

v22 God's compassions never fail.

v 33 For he does not willingly bring affliction or grief to the Children of men.

v 40 Let us examine our ways and test them and let us return to the Lord.

v 52 Hunted like a bird...called to God from the pit. He comes and redeems the life.

Hosea 11 God loves Israel as a child. Leads with cords of human kindness and ties of love . He lifted the yoke and bent down to feed them. His children come like doves. (Picture of a caretaker of birds and puppies)

Amos 3:1-15 We only get caught if a snare has been set.

v7 Surely the Lord does nothing without revealing it to his servants the prophets.

v8 The Sovereign has spoken, but who can prophecy?

Prov 1 Useless is a net spread in full view. God's prophecy is his view. Insight, prudence, knowledge, discretion, discerning, guidance....listen to God. Problems are waywardness and complacency. They bring destruction.

Rev 18 Demons likened to unclean birds. Babylon is a cage for unclean birds. It is to fall. It was a cage for bodies and souls of men held by its magic spell. Babylon is to be destroyed.

Matt 8:20 Jesus says that birds have nests. Specific nest for a specific bird.

Matt 13:31 Kingdom of Heaven is like a mustard seed which grows up and the birds build their nest. God provides his birds with freedom within His Kingdom principles.

Luke 9:58 Jesus does not have a nest. A nest is to be for a season.

Rom 1:18 Birds represent truth. Cage is suppression to the truth by wickedness.

Be TV

Words: *Sit in God's presence and display his love to others.*

The dream: *A man with large television antennas tied to himself all over. These are the antennas that are used on top of houses.*

Receive: To gather, to lay hold of; seize, to contain, to take, to find, to lift up, welcome, , take back, to bring, share, to receive to one's self, to have place for; contain.

To gather, take in, lay hold of and welcome the presence of God and pay out, share and bring that love to others. The presence of God brings his love; to you, in you, through you.

Antenna: a system of wires for transmitting or receiving electromagnetic waves.

Television: The transmission of continuous visual images as a series of electrical impulses or a modulated carrier wave, restored to visual form on the screen of a receiver, often accompanying sound.

Coming Through Closed Doors

Walls. Sometimes people think that a door is locked, or they have a wall in front of them. Actually they are the ceiling, not the wall. You reach the wall when you go as far as your vision can take you. Then you need to cash it in for a new vision. The pillars hold up the Church. If a pillar is in one of the adjacent rooms, and needs to be moved, then it must be turned sideways and carried into the main sanctuary to be stood upright again. You have to lay down your vision for the Church to be movable into the main sanctuary. (Revelation 3:12) The Church pillars hold up the vision. If the pillar is too short, it is of no use to the building. The pillar is made of the core of the tree. Center cut and needs to be vertical to have the maximum strength and use.

Maybe you think you are a cross-member and God really wants to use you as a pillar. If you hang onto the things of the past and try to mix them with God's new vision it doesn't work. You will feel like you have hit a wall. His vision will be the largest vision you can have. What are the needs for you that God sees? He looks from the top down. Tear the ceiling off your vision and allow God to impart to you and put His ceiling on it. If you reach a wall, what do you do? Look for the door first. If it is locked, then put yourself down (humble yourself and place your vision at His feet). We have already been given the keys, so search yourself and your purse. What have you brought with you that is holding you back? If there is no door, then turn aside, not back. God longs to move us with His hands, not heavy equipment. The master builder has the plans for His Church and knows where the columns need to be placed. They are all based on the foundation in Him and revelation of His word to the individual. Following the wrong vision will lead you to Max out on your resources and when they stop and your vision continues there will not be a closed door, but a wall without a door, a ceiling. How do you know? Alignment with Him.

Direction for Ministry
The Shine

The Dream: *There is a car with flip up headlights. One of them is up and the other one isn't.*

The direction that God provides to us is not for our feet like a camper with a flashlight on a trail. The path that he lights for us is for eternal direction within the Kingdom of God. He is more concerned with eternal issues than with temporal issues.

He isn't here to tell us what to do, but what to do with what he has given us. It's not an outward direction, but an inward direction. Motivation will direct us. When we are motivated by the Love of God for others, we will be directed in all of our steps because they can't be wrong. Whether we step to the right or the left, people will be blessed through the ministry God has given you. Let the ministry direct you.

God will reveal his will to us from his Holy Spirit into our heart. Our spirit needs to be taught how to listen to our heart as it communes with God. Then, when he talks to us, we should cherish those words. Write them down and ask him to help us understand them. What do they mean? Only he can interpret what he has put on our hearts. God will enlighten us, we don't have to try to do it on our own. Just ask him. It only takes as long as it does for us to blink, for God to reveal his vision to us. It is like shutting our eyes then opening them again. When we open them, we see with his sight, not our own.

We can ask for wisdom and understanding. God has provided us a window through a relationship with Jesus Christ to know his ways for us.

He will not reveal his will for us to our mind. Our mind needs to be taken out of the loop. What God tells our heart to do provide the radiance to us. It makes us shine with his light.

Our heart needs to be pure for God to shine his glorious light into it. We cannot allow anything to impede this purity. We must get rid of anything that blocks the light. When he points out sin in our life, take care of it. We need to listen closely to his words. Guard the purity of God's words in our heart and do not mix them with impure thoughts.

Everyone has hearts with eyes. The eyes of their heart see into our eyes. Like two cars meeting; our headlights flash at one another. When our eyes shine with the Love of God to others, they will see him as they look into our eyes. The Holy Spirit that God has instilled in us will be seen when we look at them. God shines with his love, as we Love others by using the ministry he has given us.

When we get the eyesight that God has intended, he will make our steps to be faithful to his plan. He never gets tired of providing us with his direction and the empowerment to do it. When we look to him, the path will seem like we aren't even touching the ground. No rocks will make us stumble. We won't get tired because he will continue to renew us with his strength.

Following his voice within our heart will continue to

inspire us in his direction. This will provide direction to others as well. Then we will be able to give cups of cold water to his children, because we will have it to give.

We can't draw water out of a well that we don't have.

Genesis 3:5, Psalms 19:8, 119:18, Proverbs 4:20-25, 7:2,15, Isaiah 29.10, 40.26, 52.8-15, Matthew 5.29, Luke 11:34, I Corinthians 2:9, 15:52, Ephesians 1:18, 6:6, Colossians 3:22

Spirit Dominated

The Word pierces between our soul and spirit. The word of God is living and active and sharper than any two-edged sword and piercing as far as the division of soul and spirit, of both joints and marrow, and able to judge the thoughts and intentions of the heart (Hebrews 4:12). We are divided into three parts: Soul (Mind), body and Spirit.

Soul: The inner part of a person that permits life. The soul enables the person to have life; to live. (Genesis 1:27). It is the difference between life and death of an individual. There can be warm flesh, but it is not alive without God making it a soul. A soul is what makes people eternal beings. We are all eternal and enter into damnation or glory after we pass from this earth. It is not a question of if we have eternal life, but where we will spend it. Our soul is the self drive of appetites and desires. (Deuteronomy 12:20) (Jeremiah 13:7).

Spirit: The Spirit within us permits us to walk. It is the activating force within living being. Notice in Genesis that God Breaths into Adam the breath of life. This is the spiritual aspect of Adam being born. (Genesis 2:7). But, it is the spirit in man and the Breath of the Almighty gives them understanding (Job 32:8). It's about the breath; it is the wind which provides movement to the walk (John 3:8). The spirit of us is the life center retained by God.

No man has authority to restrain the wind with the wind, or authority over the day of death: (Ecclesiastes 8:8). You (God) hide your face, they are dismayed: You take away their spirit, they expire (Psalms 104:29). The spirit of a man dominates our moral character (Proverbs 16:18, Hosea 4:12). The spirit of an individual is the source of one's insight. Jesus knew the hearts of those around Him by discerning with His spirit (Mark 2:8). Man's spirit can know his thoughts. For who among men knows the thoughts of a man except the spirit of the man which is in him? Even so the thoughts of God no one knows except the Spirit of God.(I Corinthians 2:11)

Can be dominated by Holy Spirit through new birth

When we become children of God through belief in Jesus Christ as our Savior, we become sensitive to inner voice of Holy Spirit. We receive a spirit of adoption as sons by which we cry out "Abba! Father! (Rom 8:15). This new adoption enables us to think spiritually dominated by God. The Spirit Himself (God's Holy Spirit) testifies with our spirit that we are children of God. (Romans 8:16). The same new spirit gives mind of Christ to believer (I Corinthians 2:16). You are renewed in the spirit of your mind when you have the new spirit. You get the disposition of Christ including His righteousness and holiness (Ephesians 4:23).

Can be dominated by an evil spirit. When Saul disobedient to God while he was anointed King of Israel, God took His Spirit from him and an evil spirit terrorized him (I Samuel 16:14-16). Saul was living a life of disobedience, so God's presence departed from him. Never assume once you are freed from your sins, you are free to be disobedient and will not suffer harm for it. God has called us to live a life of continued seeking after righteousness through daily forgiveness by the blood of Jesus covering our sins.

Prayer without Guidance

Good prayer Vs best prayer. It is possible to have God directed prayer. Take for instance, that I want to meet you at a restaurant. If I get there before you, I can order for you. If I don't ask you what you want, I may not order what you like. Perhaps, if I know you well enough, I can predict what you will eat, but I will not be as good as if you ordered it yourself. When we have an opportunity to ask God what he wants for our prayer before we pray it, it is similar to asking him what he would want us to order for him from the restaurant. If we ask, then pray what he tells us to, then he will do it for sure because we will have prayed 'into' his will. Prayer that is directed by God is the best. It is on target.

'Can Do' Prayer

Often when we come to God, we have ideas of what we want from him or for him to do. These prayers are directed by us. We direct the prayer time. There is a barrage of questions asked of him without expecting the answer to appear except within the circumstances being changed that we are praying for. This is not interactive prayer. It is one sided. Kind of like an interrogation of God without giving him time to answer. Here are some examples of 'can DOS' that we pray.

Can you hear me, God? (Are you there? Do you exist for real?)

Can you be called on by man? (is it possible to have a relationship with you while I am still on the earth?)

What Can you do for me God? (Why would this relationship be needed for me? What do you have to offer me outside of what I already have?)

Can you do this? (Is it possible?)

Can you do this for me? (Is it your will for Me?)

Can I have this? (Does he want it for Me. Am I worthy?)

What Can I do? (Is there something I am not doing?)

Canned prayers. (Rote prayers. 'Our Father')

Canned prayers. (Do you always come into His presence the same way? Do you honestly think he is listening? Would you say the same thing to someone all the time if you thought they were listening?)

Canned prayers. Are we saying the same thing over and over? Why?

We think that if we are persistent He will listen. He is like a stubborn old man who will finally give in if we keep on bugging him. What is a fervent prayer of a righteous man?

It's a rainbow

If we claim a few promises, then those colors will show to God. The more promises of His Word we claim, the more colors will be displayed to him. We don't know, without asking him which colors are needed for the fulfillment of the promise to be in acted by Him. When there is the right mixture of Colors, the bow will be displayed. It is external evidence of a covenant relationship between us and God. There is always a covenant, but there is not always the outward display of it. When we want an outward display of His covenants toward us, we ask. We say, "God, you love me, can you show it to me?" You can even continue to pray after the covenant is displayed! And there will be more colors. More display of his power and light!

Problems in prayer

There may be prayers that are not answered because our motivation is wrong. Do we challenge God to do something? Or maybe we are unstable. Do we pray one way one day and another way the next because we aren't sure what God wants and don't want to be found without the answer being prayed in by us? This is 'pride' in prayer.

Often we see our prayer line going into a ditch instead of before the throne room of God. Do we feel it is going down instead of up? Maybe we are following the designs of other men for prayer instead of God sent designs? Are we drawn to other people, like the prayer group, to pray, or are we drawn to God first, and then caused to pray? When God is on the other end of the line, he will draw us. We should not be pulled to him. by our needs and requests but by our relationship with him. If we allow God to come to us first, then he will well up in us and drive our prayers.

Is our prayer life turned off and on like a light? Do we go in and out of prayer time? God longs to be with us continually. He doesn't just want us to pray at our times of convenience that have been preset. We don't come to Him, but open ourselves to allow Him to come to us. Sup with us.

God says that we can test him in prayer. If we are willing to throw out big prayers, he is willing to answer them. We need only pray into his will. Sometimes we put our own sinkers on our line to God. We curse the prayers without knowing because we don't believe that God is actually listening.

Prayer needs to be met at the point of entry for the problem. We can pray around and around, but until we go through the gate, we will not gain entrance into the city. We have to find the key to the door. All the keys have been given to us! Jesus has entrusted to us the keys the

Kingdom of Heaven. We need to learn how to use them.

Sometimes we are standing in the way of the answer. We need to reach out for it but don't know how. We may be praying one direction when God wants to answer a totally different direction.

God wants to bring light into our darkness. He doesn't want our prayer closet to be dark. He wants us to know how to get the answers to our prayers. He has provided wisdom, his thoughts, for us. We don't need to tackle the problem on our own. He is available to help us. No matter how diligent and disciplined we are, if we do not pray into his will we will not be successful.

God is good. He wants nothing more than for his children to call to him and for him to respond back.

Guided Prayers

Relationship with God:

Prayer is communication with the God who created the Universe. He has been reaching out to us since He created us. He created us so he could have company, so He longs to be part of our lives. Prayer needs to flow from the relationship that you have with Him. His love for us needs to be the primary drawing force behind our relationship with him. Nothing else will enable the relationship to endure. (I Corinthians) He is the rock and we are to be chipped from that rock. We are to tap into Him, abide in Him, become like him; allow His love to flow through us, then flow back to him. This kind of bond will never be broken, not by anything, even death, because he has conquered death. The driving force is Him drawing us with his love, not us drawing him with ours. We must rely upon the Holy Spirit.

Holy Spirit direction:

We need to learn how to pray into His will. When we are filled with the Holy Spirit and allow his Word to speak through us, then We will become the breath of God. The breath of God is what moves things (Psalms 18). The Holy Spirit will be happy to provide direction to us if we let him. We need to create an environment that He can operate in. II Chronicles 6:41 (Now arise, O Lord and come to your resting place, you and the ark of your might. May your priests be clothed with salvation, and may your saints rejoice in your goodness.)... Dedication of the temple by Solomon

Willingness: We need to be open to be willing to do whatever he wants us to do.

Song of Praise in our heart: We need to have an attitude

Praise in our heart toward him. It is for his Glory that we pray, not our own.

Pursue Holiness: Holiness is the end product of our lives here on earth. We can have holiness on earth, but not without some pursuit of it.

Purity: Keep ourselves unstained from the world. We need to seek to do God's will alone apart from others.

Openness: Be open to new ideas from God.

Broken: Be separated. Allow God to speak to our Spirit, and our spirit to our soul and our soul to our flesh. Then our flesh will do what our spirit needs to do to be in line with the Spirit of God.

Easily moved: We need to become easily moved. Not firmly fixed on our own ideas.

Listen: Open our spiritual eyes and ears to see and hear what he has for us.

Obedient: Be obedient to do whatever he tells us to do.

The goal is to pray into the purposes and character of God. It is revealed in Scripture, words of God in prophecy, dreams, visions, voice of God, revelations in His creation. We seek guidance from the Holy Spirit. It is to be alone and in unity with others. God will speak back to us

Pray the way God tells you to

To petition: Daniel 6:11: When Daniel learned of the bad news toward the kingdom, he went up and prayed openly on his porch.

Pray because it is the right thing to Do, not because of any rules men make. Pray in the openly to God in the right direction, on your knees.

He continued doing something that God had told him to do. Go the same direction until God says, turn.

Wrong attitudes we bring to prayer

Being too casual before God: Seek relationship with

God as a child who is in need of a mediator because we are sinners and He has paid the ransom to remove our feet from the shackles. We are considered enemies of God without repentance. We should never think we can come casually into the presence of God. {Job 33:26}

An attitude against the person we are praying for:
Moses was a chosen leader by God, so he had the authority to speak for the people. He had to put himself completely into God's hands to be used to lead the people.

The people grew impatient and spoke against God and against Moses. Then the Lord sent venomous snakes among them...Then they came to Moses and said, " We have sinned when we spoke against you and God. Pray that the Lord will take the snakes away...So Moses prayed for the people. Then the Lord told him what to do.
He made a bronze snake. Put it on a pole and had the people look at it. The were healed. Numbers 21:4-9

He had to put his own attitudes aside
Entreat God
Wait for instructions from God,
Believe the answer God had given him
Act on what God told him to do
Spend his energy for another who had wronged him: Sacrifice Himself for another
Convey the message to the people so they would be healed.
They had to look to the healer.

When God comes to you with a problem:

Deuteronomy 9:14 God told him that the people had become corrupt, turned away from what he had commanded them and cast an idol for themselves. He says, "Let me alone, so that I may destroy them, and blot out their name...and make a nation of you."

This time:
God tells him there is a problem
Moses goes to the people first
Becomes angry and throws down the tablets
He turns to God in prayer prostrate 40 days
Because he fears the anger and wrath of the Lord
He knew how mad God was.... mad enough to change the whole plan and not include them in any of it.
Then he prays for them...special prayer for Aaron
He does what God tells him to do
Burns the calf in the fire, crushes it up, puts it in the stream that flows to the people.
God instructs him to make another tablet

God asked him not to pray because he knew that Moses could change his mind. He knew that if Moses prayed, he would be gracious and forgive the people. God may tell you of a problem that needs to be fixed. The proper response isn't to go fix it. You will mess it up more. He became angry. Because he was angry, he did not avoid God, but spent time in fasting to try to get himself out of the middle of the situation. Then he entreats God and God tells him what to do. The results of the sin still flows to the people, but God's wrath is stayed. God forgives Moses' anger and tells him how to replace what has been broken.

Prayer from the heart is blessed

I Sam 1: Hannah prayed for the baby Samuel:
She went to where God was: The temple
Sought him with the bitterness of her soul

Weeping

Made a deal with God if he gives the child to her, she will give him back to God. (God makes deals)

She kept on praying. Persistent

Poured out her soul to the Lord

God used Eli to bless her prayer into action

Hannah met God where she was. She was in an anguished state. She went to where he was, she didn't try to bring him to her. She went to the Temple. She poured out her heart to him and he responded to her prayer with an answer of God's blessing.

The dream:

Bev, a new Christian is in a walk-in closet. She has a fishing pole and is fishing in a small well.

I come into the closet and ask her, " What are you doing?"

She says," I'm a fishin'. There's a fish in there, and I'm gonna catch um."

I look into the ditch. There is a healthy full grown trout swimming around. The only other thing in the hole is a tin can. She is fishing for all she is worth. Very diligently trying to catch this fish with her fishing pole.

Then, it's like her time is up for the day and she says, "Well, that's it for today, I will be back tomorrow...and I will catch that fish."

Interpretation:

Many of us think that prayer is done in a 'closet'. We do our praying in the dark without direction from God. We base our prayers on 'fishing' for what God might want for us. We wonder if we 'can' do things and if he 'can' do things. We preserver without direction.

Obedience brings Healing

Our obedience will lead to healing. We need to be following the Doctor's orders to receive healing within the body of Christ on earth. We need to learn to listen and follow him.

Even though, we have been found to be noncompliance patients, the Great Physician will bring healing to us because there have been others who have gone before us that have asked for it. They have mourned our sickness and cried out to the Father in behalf of us.

The way that God will bring healing to a people that refuse to listen to him, is to put a mirror up to our face. He shows us our sin and we become sick of it. The Holy Spirit is God's mirror to us to reflect the image of God to us. He shows us who we really are; that we are indeed sick and in need of a Physician.

Then, after he shows us who we really are, he continues to reveal himself to us showing the other side of the Holy Spirit; Comfort. It is like seeing the backside of the mirror. It is paper that can be pealed off. When the paper is pealed off (our blackness of sin taken away) we are allowed to look through the glass to see what God has for us. The black paper is Satan's written decrees against us; all of the slander that he brings up to tear us down. It is the blackness that his kingdom brings. When God shows up, he tears down the kingdom of the enemy because it is exposed. It is pealed off with his forgiveness which is offered through Jesus Christ.

Then, when we see our sin and our need for a savior, we turn from our own ways and seek the orders from the Physician to receive our healing. The Angels sing, the Father sings, the Spirit sings. Our spirit sings in tune with God's Holy Spirit for the first time ever. We become singers for God, to sing his praise. We are thankful for his healing.

The result of the new healing is peace. We receive calmness within ourselves. What was once a war between our flesh, soul and spirit has now been ended. The soul that was created to praise God was set against the flesh whose desire was to praise itself. The flesh was at war with our spirit and the soul was stuck in the middle. There was no peace. When our body becomes unified, we receive peace because we are now unified.

The same is true with the body of Christ. Because of the prayers that have gone before, God is planning to unite his Body, the Church, with his Holy Spirit through the will of the Father. The only thing that stands in the way is our will; our soul. The flesh of the Body of Christ, his church needs to become unified to be able to be touched by the Great Physician to be healed. They need to become completely obedient to his orders. Only He knows how the pieces are to be assembled, so we need to follow his instructions for assembly.

Isa 57:18-19

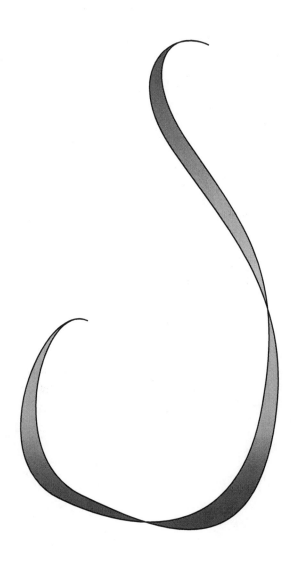

Section 2

Character of Prophetic Prayer

Training into the Gifts

God wants me to build our training on an eternal track; His love. We cannot fit our old training from the world into the new training that God wants to give us for the Kingdom of God. God's training is moving. What He taught you several years ago was good for then; but now He wants to teach you something new. We need to be open to learn new things from Him. We have a new family. Our Father wants to train us.

Our training will come when we put on the shoes that He has prepared to fit us. We need to pick the gift He has given us and use it to train us. When we put on His righteousness, He gives us shoes to walk in His Kingdom. His training will make us ready to receive the Good News that Jesus gives His people peace. We have peace within ourselves, peace with one another and peace with God. He will teach us how to share that peace with others to promote His Kingdom the way it is supposed to be promoted.

We don't have to walk alone. God has given us transportation to live within this world. God wants to give us our vehicle to share the Good News with others. He wants to move within His Children to bring healing, restoration and peace. He will give us access to His mind and His plans.

When we us our gifts from the Holy Spirit, others will say, "Only God could have known this. I declare God is alive today. Praise Him!"

We all need to be trained to hear God's voice. We can sacrifice ourselves for the service of God, but without His word of direction, there is no way to know whether the sacrifice was for others, ourselves or God. The Church has gone through an extended period of self denial. They are tired. They have given away themselves hoping they will receive a reward, but none has come. They have given up on getting any reward here on earth and think that the only reward will be in heaven

But they do not know how to let God examine their hearts and tell them whether or not the service was one that He wanted. They picked one that they thought God would like, or one that someone else told them to do. God has been silent to them.

Some have given their tokens to pay others to do the work of God. They are hoping on the prayers and spiritual guidance of others to get them into right standing with God. Many have put their trust in their leaders just like a driver of a bus. They are hoping that the driver has read the map, will follow the signs of God collecting enough tokens from them to get the (bus load) whole congregation into the place where God wants them.

We need to learn how to look out the front window to heaven for ourselves to see the road. When we spend time in prayer and the presence of God He will teach us His ways. He will teach us the difference between His Kingdom and the Kingdom of this world. We will learn about God when we put effort into it. He has a job for us within His Kingdom. We need to ask Him about it. (See the Steps in the Garden-a set of books by Sheri Hauser more information on growing in the gifts of the spirit.)

God wants to move His people from the Gifts of prophecy on to other gifts within the body. He wants to free us to become what He created us to be: To train us as a child in Christ. Before we protected our own interests, but our Heavenly Father wants us to protect others for their sake. We need to lay down our selfish desires.

When we learn how to hear His voice, then He will lead us in other areas of ministry. We need to be put into motion.

The Holy Spirit tells us what to do and we must become obedient to it. There is a lab with this course. There is mental and physical discipline when learning from God. His words sometimes come in riddles. We have to search for the meaning. Then, sometimes He asks us to do hard things like pray for extended times. This can be very tiring physically, but that is part of the discipline that will lead to Holiness in our life. He will give us grace to do the job He gives us to do. But we have to ask for it.

In relation to the gifts, we, the students, should be like our Great Teacher if we are doing things right. We will learn and use them with a spirit of servant-hood. We must learn how to dispense that which is entrusted to us with meekness. God is calling us to become willing and obedient to follow Him. Growing into our spiritual gifting is our obedience demonstrated.

He wants to use us within the body of Christ to prune the other trees. The Scripture says: As Iron sharpens iron, so one man sharpens another. When we are sensitive to Him, He will use us as His hands to help teach others. When the Children of God get the training that He intends for us, His robe of righteousness will fill His temple. He will train us to live in His righteousness. He adorns us with His training and it will fill the temple and glorify Him.

The unification of the Spirit is accomplished through the Bond of Peace; His peace to us, in us, through us. God wants to train us to become peace keepers not warriors. We need to stop fighting the Devil and declare the victory.

Psalms 68:18, Proverbs 22:6, Isaiah 2:4, 6:1, Micah 4:3, Ephesians 4:8, I Timothy 4:7, Titus 2:4.

Hitching Rides

You were left waiting and when he finally shows up, he has sent another. From your position, you can only see a little of what is going on with the whole thing.

But it looks like they took a connector out: it was a bridge. It's actually what they needed to pull this trailer house. Like a tow bar. I'm putting it back. It allows us to move with the Spirit being pulled by God.

Do you not know that your body is the temple of the living God. God longs to live within us helping us to become a mobile house pulled by the power of God. The connection is essential for us to be attached to God and be able to move in the Spirit world.

Hitching Trains

The Dream:

People want to hitch onto the back of the train. They want to ride this train because their uncle is the flagman. They put my old car on the back. They put their children in the car and hop in. The car doesn't fit on the tracks. The car comes off the rail and breaks it. The whole train is stopped because it is attached as a caboose. The rail is too fragile. It breaks twice. I go along for the ride watching with my shoes off. Then, I take my shoes and walk back to my car to take me home. I meet a friend from work. (I have tried to witness to her, but she is resistant to God. She is full of bitterness from life.) She lent out her car and now rides the bus. I offer her a ride not just to my house, but way across town to hers.

Interpretation:

It doesn't work to hitch someone else's' training on the back of the train that God has planned for you. We each need our own training. If we try to hitch our training onto others' lives it is like hooking a car onto a train. The track will be all wrong. The only training that is lasting is built on the love of God by himself. Sometimes we 'ride the bus' on someone else's training. They have a vision and God has trained them. We think that we can hop on their band wagon. It doesn't work. We need to help others receive their own training from God.

Heart and Lungs

The dream:
There is a patient upstairs. He has had heart surgery. A pulmonologist and a cardiac surgeon come to check on him. They come right through the front door without knocking like they have been here frequently. The patient is in good condition. He is discharged.

Interpretation:
Our body is in need of heart surgery. There has been an interruption in the flow to the heart that causes chest pain. Our heart is sick, we have a broken heart. Oxygen is not getting to our heart. The voice of God isn't getting to the heart of what matters in our life.

God wants to do laser surgery to repair the flows; the flow of His word and His voice to the people. He will come with His presence as a surgeon; use the knife of His word to pierce our chest. He wants to come through the walls of our flesh and bones to get to our heart.

His word is the oxygen that we need to survive. When we are born again to newness of life, we are to take in his word just like we are newborns learning to breath. The word, the voice of God needs to flow within the system he has built within us. The flow is by his power and direction. When the voice of God flows in the direction without resistance or obstruction it will bring life to all aspects of the body.

Many of us have been scarred by life. We have taken in harmful things that have left us scarred. God wants to heal our scars, remove the scar tissue and allow free transfer of his word/his voice to the rest of the body; As an individual and as a Church. When we have heart surgery, we are assigned a surgeon and a pulmonologist. The heart and the lungs must work in harmony; with one tone, to provide life.

When we call upon God, He will make the house call just as a physician to perform surgery on our wounded hearts. We need to look up to Him; raise our arms and voice to His praise and glory. We need to call on a higher Kingdom; the Kingdom of God to help us. We must be in a place where He can come. Repentance, humility, and openness to receive His healing are essential. We must unlock the doors to our house. Open our heart to receive His healing before He can come in. He won't come through the walls or locked doors. These locks must be opened from the inside. As often as we call on Him, the great physician will make house calls; He will come with His work (air) and His love (heart) and give us the power and direction for it to flow to the areas of our lives that need healing.

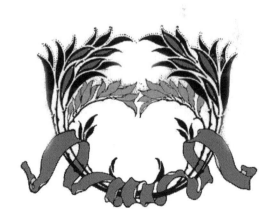

Thunder in the Word of God

Word: *God's voice is like thunder*

Interpretation:

Our spiritual eyes must be opened to see the light. But it is the voice that tells us how close his power is to us. When a storm comes, the wind has a sudden rush and then the sky becomes darkened. You can hear the thunder in the distance. When you hear the voice of God, then it should cause you to look up into the heavens, like looking for a storm. We look up to see when the rain will come. When we hear the voice of God, then we look up to see his display of power and his shower of his power into our lives.

You cannot direct thunder anymore than you can direct God's voice. The power is displayed in the ability to illuminate; to enlighten, to set afire our souls to Him. It is pure current that always strikes our highest structure goes to the ground. We reach out to Him using his rod (the Word of God) longing for his power strike. He always immediately goes to our foundation. If we are founded IN Christ, then the building is secure. His rod of righteousness must be outstretched atop the building to have the power hit it as the tallest object. We need to train our ears to hear his voice and anticipate the power of God coming to us in the form of lightening. We lift up his word, hold it up above our heads, and look for him to come along and flow through us with his current. Our foundation has to be built on our relationship with the firm Rock, Jesus.

Thunder in the Scriptures is associated with the Voice of God coming to people. It is always a group of people usually accompanied with hail, lightening and often a trumpet. Exodus 9:23 Moses stretched out his hand in Egypt and God sent hail, thunder and lightning to open the way for freedom into the promise land. Exodus 20:18: When God gives the ten commandments there were thunder, lightening, a trumpet and a mountain smoking. God was attempting to open a way to himself for the people, but they did not recognize his voice and were afraid. Why didn't Moses have any problem going into the cloud? He knew who the cloud represented. He recognized the voice of God as representing a loving God He knew the character of God to know God was into life, not death. He had experience spirit to Spirit contact with God and His hungry for God's spirit led him into the Cloud. His love for God, the desire he knew God had to want to be with him, and his desire to be with God.

The others were kept away from God because of 'fear of Death.'

Often times His voice is awesome, but his voice is always one of love, not death.

Samuel opens the way to God and God opens the way for the people to win the battle. I Samuel 7:10: The people go to Samuel and Samuel goes to God. Samuel offers sacrifice to God and while he is sacrificing, God thunders and throws the enemies into a panic. Again in I Samuel 12:18: Samuel called on God to send rain, thunder and lightning. All the people stood in awe of God and Samuel. They had asked for a king. Samuel opens the way to God then God opens the way to a kingship.

When he points his affection at us, it is overwhelming. He holds nothing back. His voice thunders in marvelous ways... he does great things beyond our understanding So that all men may know his work. He talks to the snow and the rain. At his voice my heart pounds and leaps from its place; The roar of his voice, the rumbling that comes from his mouth. He unleashes the lightening beneath the whole heaven. He gets ready to talk (rumbles) like the ruffling of the water before a wave. Then he brings enlightenment. After that comes the thunder of his majestic voice. He's an all or nothing God. He talks to the snow and the rain. His breath produces ice.

He loads the clouds with moisture; he scatters lightening. At his direction they swirl around ... to do whatever he commands. He brings the clouds to punish men, or to water his earth and show his love. God comes in awesome majesty. The Almighty is beyond our reach and exalted in power; in his justice and great righteousness, he does not oppress. The Lord opens our hearts us to himself. He shakes us, breaks us, twists us, and brings us down to ground level with his voice. His voice strikes our groundwork.

In Job 38: Then the Lord answered Job out of the storm. Job had darkened God's counsel with words without knowledge. He had listened to others when he should have been consulting God on the subject. God points out that man do not know the laws of the heavens. Only God alone. God opens enlightenment to himself. Then when God sends his voice within the thunder, Job says, ' my ears had heard of you, but now my eyes have seen you.'

The thunder enlightens us to his voice. Opens us up enough to hear him. God raises his voice to the clouds and covers himself with a flood of water. He sends lightning bolts and has them report to him, 'here we are.' (God knows where his voice is at all times. His voice goes out and he follows it to bring about it's purposes.) God opens our hearts to hear him and opens our mind to understand his voice. Your thunder was heard in a whirlwind, your lightening lit up the world... You led your people like a flock. God opens the way.

When we cry to God, he answers us out of the brightness of his presence the clouds advance. Hailstones and lightening. Lightening scatters and routs enemies. The valleys are exposed and the foundations laid bare. At the blast of the breath of your nostrils. Then he reaches down at takes hold of me and draws me out of deep waters. He rescues from my powerful enemy and brings me to a spacious place because he delights in me. According to my righteousness, the cleanness of my hands. Have turned toward God. Blameless.

The voice of the Lord is over the waters; the God of glory thunders, the Lord thunders over the mighty waters. The voice of the Lord breaks the cedars. The voice of the Lord shakes the desert, twists the oaks, and strips the forests bare. Then he can give strength to his people and bless his people with peace. His voice opens up our needs.

In Revelation, the voice of God is associated with opening doors. Rev 4, the door to heaven was open: The Throne of God in heaven has flashes of lightening, rumblings and peals of thunder. There is the Opening of first of seven seals. The opening of the 7th seal is the prayers of the saints, incense on the golden altar before God. Then the angel takes the censer and fills it with fire from the altar and then hurls it on the earth there comes peals of thunder, rumblings and flashes of lightening and an earthquake. (Incense: Wood burned to produce a pleasant odor.)

Then, at the end times, God's temple is opened in heaven followed by more thunder. The Lamb stands on

Mt Zion and sings a new song before God. At Armageddon the angel pours out his bowl into the air and declares, "It is done!"

In response, the saints sound like thunder praising God at the wedding of the Lamb. His bride has made herself ready.

>Job 28:25, 37, Psalms 18, 29:3, 77:18,
>Revelation 4:5, 6:1, 8:5, 14:1, 16:18,16:18.

Character of a True Prophet

God's goal is to rise up a prophet who will do whatever is on His mind and heart. Only to say what He tells them to, no more, no less. A message is entrusted to one that is chosen by God. Though David was a man after God's heart, God did not speak to him through visions and dreams, but spoke through Nathan to him. The vision is sealed until God releases it to someone with a heart near to God to be able to understand it.

The person has to be pure, Holy, humble and needy. A vision is called 'altar hearth' or Ariel. The individual has to be ready to come near the heat of the altar of God. The priest has to be astounded with wonder upon wonder as the Holiness of God is displayed while the scroll is opened. The individual stands in the council of God. They are to be alert 24 hr. a day. They cry out to the Lord on behalf of His Daughter, the Church. Filled with the Holy Spirit and Power, prophets each have a station; a watch that they tend. They are to be alert and report what they see. Prophets are to look to see what God says and make it plain so that a messenger may run with it; attentive to the ear of God. They have a willingness to be quiet before Him recognizing that He whispers.

When the voice of God comes to the prophet, it will pierce his soul, motivate to call for more grace and increase their prayer life. The prophet needs to be obedient to the vision for themselves and to say it to others. He needs to be attentive to the timing for the release of the vision. Some are for now, and some for later. It there is doubt, God will tell you again as He told Peter 3 times the same vision. They praise God in their Lives.

The Spiritual Gifts within the Church
Our Crowns

A relationship with God, the Father through Jesus Christ comes with crowns. God, the Father is King of Kings, so when we become one of his children, we become joint heirs the Kingdom of God. We become heir to the Crown. He doesn't wait until we die, however to crown us, he desires to crown us now. A crown is a symbol of a position within a kingdom. God has offered us not only symbols, but position now through his grace. He wants to give us directions to run the Kingdom, but we need to learn to listen to him.

To learn about our 'crown' within the Kingdom, we need to ask the King. He will tell us where we belong; where our domain is.

We need to spend time with him in prayer and reading the Bible. He will speak to our heart about himself. He will develop a binding relationship with us; it is bound with his cords of love. We need to allow ourselves to be drawn in and bound to his love.

To forward his Kingdom, he writes his messages on the hearts of his servants. We become his message seen and read by all men. This is the way he displays his love to the world; through the messages given to us as we send them to others. He will give each of us an issue that is 'pressing' on him. With this issue, he will press on us; He will give us inner motivation to display that particular message to others through the spiritual gifts that he has given to the individual.

He will carve his name when he enters the secret place of our heart. His words inscribe. He pushes his points into us like a tattoo and etches out a message. When our heart has been washed clean by the blood of Jesus, it becomes like a tablet; a clean and white surface for a message to be written on. He tells our heart what to do. Then, when we listen to our heart, we tell our head what to think in accordance to the will of God revealed to us. This is how we are driven by our love for him. His love will drive our minds and, consequently, our lives.

When the message is etched on our heart, it must be transferred into the ministry that he has given us to be able to give it to others.

The true ministry of God works through hearts, not heads. When we allow ourselves to follow our heart with our minds, He provides grace for us to do what he asks.

When the servants of God start acting within their gifting listening to their hearts instead of their minds, God will usurp the kingdom of Satan here on earth. The Children of God will take territory from the enemy they never thought possible.

When we step into the gifts that he has for us and call upon his grace, then his supremacy rules and the Kingdom of God will triumph in every situation. The Lord has chosen to rule his Kingdom through his Children, his royal heirs. Our voice becomes his voice when we step into the realm of the Spiritual Kingdom of God. We become princes and princesses. We have been given authority through our relationship with him.

Satan has a crown of pride that he rules his kingdom with. God's crowns will overthrow the crowns of Satan when we call upon the power of God to come against the power of Satan. Then he will be turned back before he even gets in the door. We only need to rest in the gifting he has given us, his promises, and the Power of the Holy Spirit. Then watch his kingdom overcome.

When your spiritual gifting is mature, as often as you are willing, God will further his kingdom through you. You will become to the enemy like an overwhelming scourge that sweeps by. There is sheer terror to the enemy because God rises up through the gifting in his people.

As often as you use these gifts, the Kingdom of God will be forwarded. Every time without fail the battle will be won by God. It happens through the grace of God working in you with the power of the Holy Spirit. It will be strange to you. But any covenant with death is automatically annulled when you use the gift. You claim God's dominion; his crown.

When we form alliance with his Kingdom, he will use us to free those bound without hope. We proclaim to others freedom, comfort, deliverance, salvation, and all the riches of the Kingdom of God through the ministry he calls us to. He wants to use us to sound his victory trumpet to rescue those is despair. Each of us are given a message to communicate to others. It is our responsibility to discharge the trust that has been committed to us. We long to have Jesus say that we have been faithful servants, to enter into the joy that has been set aside for us. When we pay attention to his voice, he will tell us what to do in each step of our walk and in the lives of others. God will counsel us with his eye upon us as a father would a child.

Words: *We wait until everyone is at the table, then we focus on the gifts.*

Zechariah 9:16, Proverbs 4.9, Isaiah 8:18, 28, 6, Matthew 27;29, I Corinthians 9, I Thessalonians 2.19, II Timothy 4.8, James 1.12, I Peter 5.4 Revelations 2.10. Hebrews 2.7, Proverbs 14.17

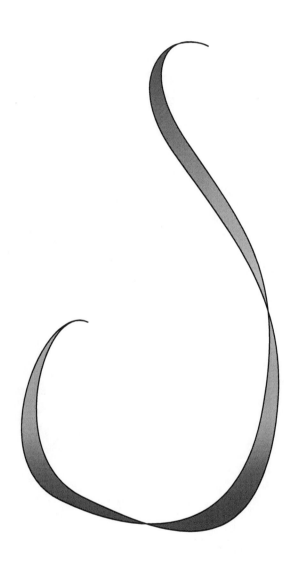

Section 3

Hearing from God Many Ways

True Prophecy

The dream or vision has to be interpreted to be a revelation. Then its purpose is to pour out a Spirit of Grace and Supplication. To expose sin and ward off captivity of God's people. He brings council and understanding of Himself. His purpose is for his people to grow in knowledge and be fruitful for His Kingdom; to bring restraint to the people. The revelations provide bumpers on the side of the road as they travel down the road toward the coming of Jesus Christ. The visions declare His Holiness as we see his prophecy fulfilled in our children. Forward action of His Kingdom is demonstrated in signs and wonders. True prophecy calls for a change.

Prophecy

Prophecy is words from God. It is God's words for us today.

'Prophecy imparts the express purpose of God in our current situations. Teaching shows us the mind of God, while prophecy often reveals His heart. p 18. *Developing your Prophetic Gifting by Graham Cooke*

'To put it simply, the Bible gives strategy, while prophecy reveals tactics. p19. Prophecy brings us, by direct verbal communication, into contact with God's real perspective on our lives and current situations. Prophecy inspires understanding of mysteries and knowledge (p29 Cooke)

Types of Prophecy

Wigglesworth notes: P102 Prophecy by the power of the Holy Spirit has power to bring to light and open understanding of the heart.

Kinds of prophecy:

- *Testimonial prophecy*: Your testimony of 'Jesus saved Me' (All have this)

- *Anointed prophecy*: For prophetic utterance; illumination of truth by the word of life.

- *Gift of prophecy*: Brings anointing, fire, confirmation, and utterance until those who hear are moved.

Caution not to use it unless the power of the Holy Spirit is upon you and you have an intense thirst. You are to stop talking when He says stop, and to go when He says go. You are not heard because of many words, but because you are definite. The Spirit is manifested in order: Comfort, exhortation, edification.

The difference between Knowledge, prophecy and wisdom is that knowledge is information which the individual would not have known unless given from God. Prophecy pulls in the power of the Word. Wisdom is thinking from God's perspective. Someone with the gift of wisdom uses scriptures to answer life's questions.

Let me give an example to help understand the difference. (See the series of books Steps in the Garden for in depth understanding of the Gifts, calling and anointing of the Holy Spirit in an individual's life.)

Let's say, for instance someone comes up to the altar for prayer. The one doing the praying seeks no information from the one requesting prayer, but calls on God to provide what is needed.

An individual operating with the gift of knowledge might say, "You have a deep pain in your foot and God wants to heal it."

Someone operating with the gift of wisdom might say, "Call upon Me you who are heavy laden and I will give you rest. My yoke is easy and my burden is light. I see you are heavy laden and very tired from your walk. Let's call on God."

Someone operating with the gift of prophecy might say, "The trouble caused you, you suspect is from someone you love, but it is sent from the enemy. Rebuke him and he will flee."

Note that all three gifts gathered information from a source other than themselves. They had to hear the voice of God and assimilate it to help meet the person who needed prayer. Quite simply Prophecy is the ability to hear the voice of God, knowledge is information on what is wrong while Wisdom is how to fix the problem.

So, you see, the foundation of all of the spiritual gifts is the gift of prophecy. How can you fix something without knowing what the problem is or what the solution is? You need to first, hear the voice of God, then put together the pieces to fix the problem.

Developing your Prophetic Gifting by Graham Cooke
Word of Knowledge opens up the issue (info about someone)
Word of prophecy speaks God's heart into it
Word of wisdom tells us how to respond to the heart of God.
The person who would receive this gift has to understand the grace and goodness of God. The visions of a prophet are to lift the congregation to see where God is taking them. It is a building ministry. The vision is created through prayer. True prophecy is concerned with morality of the work; Holiness that is God's heart. *(P 148 Cooke)*

Categories of Prophetic Words
Different categories of Prophetic words

Forth telling is declaring the word of the Lord, communicating the heart of God for the present. This declaration can come via teaching, preaching, the spoken prophetic word, vision and interpretation and symbolic acts. It will exhort, edify and console as well as admonish, provide warning and bring reproof (Rev 2-5).

Another aspect of the prophetic role is predictive prophecy, called foretelling. This is communicating the future as it is perceived in the heart and mind of God. This is used to shape the direction of the church; to cause a desire for godliness; to empower and release people.

1. Confirming word: Establish strengthen people in what they know is right. Resay to people what they already know.

2. Future Word: Maps out the course

3. New Word: No link to the present. May be distant future. Long term vision. *(P 150 Cooke)*

Progression of the Gift

Gift of prophecy is defined as going into a swimming pool. The individual can be any where along the deepness. The maximum depth in the relationship with God correlates with the Office of Prophet gift. *(Cooke P159)*

Levels of gifting
1. *Inspirational prophecy-* encourages, builds up and comforts people. (All should have this level of prophecy no matter what other gifts they have)

2. *Prophetic ministry-* deeper expression of the heart of God. These individuals are Brick Layers. *(Cooke P160).* Provides specific direction. Brings God's perspective, releases vision and calling and undermines the enemy. One hand on the past and one hand on the future with help from God to see people through.

3. *Office of Prophet- (Cooke P162)* Concerned with the holiness and purity and seeking to prepare the Bride of Christ. There's goal is to build the Church and establish the Kingdom values and practices for Christ's return. The prophet has a Kingdom perspective that will motivate the Church Universal towards a practical unity of the Spirit.

New Testament Prophet

The role of the Prophet in the Old Testament gave guidance to people who came looking for a word from the Lord. The New Testament prophet gives confirmation of God's word to the people. Guidance is to be through their relationship with God. He has a building ministry working with the apostles to lay foundations and establish the Church.

The prophet acts as a catalyst within the Church; he make things happen. God is full of plans and purposes for His Church. A prophet will envision and call the Church and individuals into an understanding and receipt of those plans and purposes. God still reveals His secrets to His servants the prophets. The prophet provides illumination for the Church to the voice of God.

A true revelation will always cause a revolution. There are many words that must be fulfilled before Christ's return, and we will need prophetic revelation to interpret those signs. Prophets are making a people prepared for the Lord (Isa 40:3). They are working to prepare for the second coming of Christ. Part of that preparation is receiving and imparting of specific revelation. Where there are credible and active prophets, the Church will not stumble in ignorance. A prophet must interpret the signs correctly.

The role of the NT prophet is to train people:

- To hear the Lord for themselves
- Teach believers to find and live the will of God for themselves
- Instruct and train in the gifts of prophecy
- Bring the words of God by inspired teaching and utterance.
- Impartation of the gifts of the Holy Spirit.

Interrelationship with the other ministries

NT prophet is to work under authority of the apostolic ministry. There should be a working relationship to provide adequate check and balances for both ministries. NT prophet acts as a catalyst within the Church; they make things happen. They are the eyes of the body of Christ. They see things ahead of others. They should notice when the Holy Spirit is about to show up at a meeting. They should also notice when the enemy is at a meeting.

In personal experience, those with the gift of prophecy are the first to stand, the first to kneel and the first to begin to get restless in a congregation. They are like a guard dog to a pack of sheep. They notice a stir in their spirit and the Holy Spirit gives them a message. They begin to pray and act upon that message. They might discern the presence of an evil spirit in the midst. They recognize it and kick it out (in the spiritual realm). Many times it is not the role of those with prophetic vision to pray over people or do deliverance, but to stand on the sidelines praying for those who are directly involved with the individuals who need help.

Pastors generally operate with apostolic or pastoral gifting while those with prophetic gifting provide back up for the service. However, some individuals are so gifted, it is difficult to tell which gifts they operate with. Although it is important to understand the gifts, anointing and calling of the Holy Spirit, it is not helpful to classify people. Leave that up to God.

God is full of plans and purposes for His Church. A prophet will envision and call the Church and individuals into an understanding and receipt of those plans and purposes. God still reveals His secrets to His servants the prophets. The prophet provides illumination for the Church to the voice of God. *(Cooke P 168)*

Prophets are making a people prepared for the Lord (Isa 40:3). They are working to prepare for the second coming of Christ. Part of that preparation is receiving and imparting of specific revelation to the earth.

A true revelation will always cause a revolution. There are many signs and words which must be fulfilled before Christ's return, and we will need prophetic revelation to interpret those words and signs. Where there are credible and active prophets, the Church will not stumble in ignorance. A prophet must interpret the signs correctly....and that is why this book is written...as direction to correction.

Prophets are preparing the Bride of Christ. It is this body of people that God is sanctifying and cleansing (the rite of purification), to present it with no spots, wrinkles or blemishes; A people of holiness and glory.

Prophets are activists. They are part of the equipping of the saints for the work of the service team.

Recognizing Gifting within God's people

It is interesting to note that when an anointed member of the Church discerns gifting in other people, prophecy can draw that gift to the attention of the individual.

When a apostle or prophet lays hands on people for those gifting to emerge, there is an impartation that takes place.

Currently we have a malnourished body of believers across the world because the Eph 4 ministries have not taken their rightful place in much of Christendom. These ministries equip people to be joined and knitted together by what every member is contributing. As every member is activated to be effective in the work, the church grows up (Eph4:16).

Real prophets promote ministry and have a passion to train and release others.

References

Breaking Strongholds in your city by C. Peter Wagner
Developing your Prophetic Gifting by Graham Cooke
Dreams and Visions by Jane Hamon
Ever increasing faith by Smith Wigglesworth
God's Dream Team by Tommy Tenney
Informed Intercession by George Otis Jr
The ministry of Intercession by Andrew Murray
Personal Prophecy Series (3 books) by Dr. Bill Hamon
Possessing the Gates of the Enemy by Cindy Jacobs
Prophetic intercession by Barbara Wentroble
Spiritual Gifts by Smith Wigglesworth
Victorious Warfare by Harold Caballeros
The Voice of God by Cindy Jacobs

The link between Apostles and Prophets

Apostles and prophets are clearly linked together in Scripture (Ephesians 2:20) The Prophet will see the end product in terms of the building God is erecting. The apostle as a wise master builder is gifted to build the property, line upon line and brick by brick. At every stage of the work, prophecy and wisdom will be needed to put things in their rightful place. There is a dual role of building and erecting the church and equipping and releasing the saints so that the church can be further built up. The bigger the house, the more we need to release the people.

There may be tensions in the relationship between prophets and apostles. It could indicate that something is happening. Prophets have a way of plowing up the ground and causing disturbance. Sometimes this is sorely needed. I know many pastors who, when encountering hard ground, simply lay a patio and cover everything up! Prophecy is attacking, stimulating and provoking by definition. Pastoring is about restoring calm and order. Prophets challenge; pastors soothe.

They need to talk to each other. Prophets need to brief pastors and share their burdens. Pastors should have access to prophetic revelation, not to water it down but to bring their wisdom to bear in the situation. Then together they should present a united front to the church--a partnership that should be seen and noted.

Launching Creative Miracles

You had to go to the deep water because what you have done is build a ramp for launching large vessels. They are people with unusual gifts which won't be understood or recognized as being vessels from God which carry the Holy Spirit except by those already in the deeper things of God. You have a launch ramp in that I have given you a spiritual eye to notice what others disregard or think is 'weird' as an out spout for the creativity of God.

So, I send you large vessels. And, with large vessels, either the individual must already be inside the boat operating within the gift in the Spirit recognizing it as from God, like being in a boat when it is launched, or they must get into the boat from the dock.

With large vessels you can't get into them from the shore without a lot of effort. As with the gifts which are extraordinary; waves of doctrine and strongholds of teaching will be very difficult for the person to get into the boat. You can launch their 'weird' ministry but without him getting into the boat, it will remain tied at the dock or adrift without him.

And, suppose you recognize that God has given you an unusual gift and, like a boat, you want to launch it into the deep water. And, suppose that you aren't already in the boat. How do you use the dock?

To get into a large vessel at the dock one must deny all religion, teaching, flesh and worldly values. And, lay himself on the altar of God's wisdom, forsaking all and being willing to be taught by the Holy Spirit. Otherwise, he will never be able to drive the boat. He needs lessons on how to drive this 'special' boat. With a creative miracle, it's something growing that has never been before. It is like eyes being formed into dry eye sockets; fingers where there was none and legs into hip joints which have never known legs. Creative miracles are great works of God; big vessels which must be launched into deep water otherwise they will not be under the control of the Kingdom of God.

We are talking about big displays of the manifested works of God.

What if you don't have a big creative gift, but want one.

The deal with the creative gifts is that you must be willing to learn to drive the boat. You would not think to command an aircraft carrier without training; so what makes you assume God would give you a big waterspout gift without training?

All of the individuals that I know who have big gifts received their training directly from God over a period of several years. Then, every one of them was sent to other types of training; musical, college, computer skills, voice lessons, etc. Do not assume that those you see in 'big' ministry didn't need to learn to manage money, staff development, computer skills, and a myriad of other things.

You see, there needs to be a connection between skill and learning to hear the voice of God which brings about the fruition of the release of something big.

Dealing with Different People

Words:

Turn and bite the finger. Give Him the roll and become what he wants you to be In Him. Look at those who are free next those not. Seek and find those who want to be free.

Interpretation:

There are three types of people that I encounter in this dream. There are those who want to tear me down, those who don't feel that they have any need my message, and those who know they bound by the enemy and want to be free.

Satan is the one who accuses us before others and God. God dismisses the accusations when we are honest with Him and seek forgiveness. I need to bite the finger that accuses me. Fingers are flesh. There will be those who will be jealous of us. Their flesh will mount a disagreement with us, no matter what we are doing. They are allowing their flesh to rule their thoughts. Maybe they are jealous of our ministry, or the way we love God. What ever their jealousy, it is of the flesh and the instruction from this dream is to bite that accusing finger. We don't bite the finger of the person, but the enemy. Recognize resistance within ministry as being from the enemy and pray against him.

The roll in the dream is what ever bread God gives us. He gives us Himself as the word coming down each day. We need to bring those words back to him for interpretation. When we do, He will tell us what He wants us to be. We need to be careful not to develop a ministry of running from those who are accusing us of doing bad things, but pursuing where God wants us to go. We don't need to run from the enemy. God will fight our battles. We need to bite our own flesh first, however. We need to make sure that it is not our own flesh that wants to fight others who come against us. Fasting is the only thing that helps to insure we are not using our own flesh to come against a battle of the flesh in others. For, when we fast, we beat down our own flesh and get it out of the way. Then, we can see clearly what the battle is.

We will encounter several people. There are those who want to fight us, those who want to run their own lives, and those who are asking for help. The message of this dream is to focus on those who want help and help them. Jesus said that He could only heal those who knew that they were sick. Those who know that they need a physician, seek one. Those who do not think that they are sick, will not seek help. We are to have open eyes to look for those who are asking for more of God, and to avoid those who take up our time, but are not seeking God.

Matthew 9:12, Luke 5:31

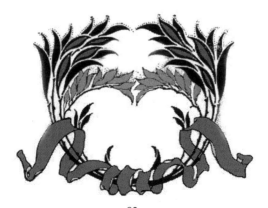

Troublemakers and Dogs

The dream:
As I am going up the stairs to my father's house, I look through the window and see dogs in the basement. I drop white duty. I let it go and it falls on the white rug. The dogs see me come and they come and try to eat it. I wrestle the dogs and throw the poop out the door with a kitten.

Interpretation:
As we walk on the path toward where we are supposed to be, we will encounter those who will cause us problems. Our Father knows they are there and is telling us to beware of them. We can look through the window that He has provided for us and see them coming. The window is the place where we see Him. We see the reflection of His voice as He speaks into our spirit with messages that cannot be heard by the enemies.

He reminds us, in this dream, that each time we release something from the Kingdom of God that we are instructed to do, the enemy will be there quickly to try to destroy it. Dogs will eat anything. That is the picture we are to get.

Dogs are, many times, stupid. I know I have had a dog that I took for a walk on the beach once. It was supposed to be a nice romantic walk with my husband on the sand. We took the dog along, thinking that He would like to get out. The walk turned into a nightmare. We couldn't keep him out of the water. He wanted to swim. Of course, all of the sand caked in his fur in the wet spots. If that was not enough, He managed to find a dead seagull to haul around and roll in. What we brought back to our hotel was a mangy, smelly dog covered with clumps of sandy mud.

God would remind us that the spiritual battles with the enemy are not a game. He is out to destroy us and Satan has an army of dogs. These dogs will try to tear up everything we do.

They don't eat it because it contains the Word of God and they cannot endure that, but they will try to rent it so that it is no good to anyone else. It is like chewing up a term paper. They don't eat it, they just destroy it, so others can't read it.

In the dream, I take what has come from me (funny picture of white poop) and throw it out the door. I toss it out the door that God provides for me. He will empower His Word to fulfill His mission. When He gives a vision and promises, He will see it through to the end.

In the dream, I toss it out the door with a kitten. A kitten is symbolic of a pet that is warm, soft and cuddly. God wants us to send His messages out with His warm heart. They should be sent out with gentleness and compassion like one would hold a kitten. He reminds us that the messages are for His children. We need to give them to the kids like we would give them a kitten.

Scripture Study: Troublemakers
There will be those within the Church who refuse to follow the directions that God gives them into their lives. They refuse to listen to their visions, their heart and their dreams. They refuse to base their ministry on the voice God directed by His love. It is not our job to expose foundations of others but to realize that any structure that is not built on the love of God will fail. We are wasting our time with them. Where there are dogs, there is dissension, discouragement, doubt, and anger within the Church.

These trouble makers will not support us that seek to listen to God for His blueprints. Some will say that our progression is too slow. They are not in tune with God's timing, but their own. They will see our potential with their eyes instead of the eyes of God. They will say that we are rebellious to leadership because we won't join the pack. Instead, they say, we want to go off on our own listening to God for ourselves. They will cause us to doubt God and His work in our lives. They will try to tear down what God is building. They will accuse us of causing dissension by listening to God on our own, seeking selfish ambition which leads to jealousy.

Psalms 22.16, 59, Jer 15.3, Ezekiel 34, Matthew 7.6, Philippians 3.2, Peter, Jude, Revelation 22.15

When Confronted with a Dog

The true prophets of God will come against the false prophets. God will allow the people to turn to the true prophets. Often they are alone because the word that God has given is unpopular. The true prophets will be slandered by the false prophets; the dogs.

It is a confrontation of the Wisdom of God verses the wisdom of men. They will mock and insult the teaching of God as senseless and silly. They will encircle us to tear apart what God has given us. They lay wait for us to conspire against us. They snarl like dogs and prowl. They put confidence in their flesh and their own wisdom.

We cannot fight them with our own strength, because they outnumber us. If we fight in their arena, they will win flesh against flesh. We cannot win the 'mind' battle and make the word of God make sense to them. God will deliver us with the Sword of His Word because it is true. We do not need to defend it, only to speak it.

When we see false prophets, we are to pray for them. As God has shown us mercy when we have doubted, we are to show them the same mercy. We are to ask God to bring down the false teaching and their nets that entrap. We should pray that their own pride be their downfall; that the curses and lies that they utter will come back to them.

When we find those false prophets that will listen to us. If we do, we are supposed to teach them about relying on the Wisdom of God and His love, rather than their own minds to interpret God's Word. To be able to minister to them, we need to get very close to be able to help them. It will arouse fear in us, because we will be afraid that we may be sucked into their logic, but if we pray for God to give us a vision of purity, then He will unravel for both of us the matrix built by Satan. He will be faithful to show the line where the flesh and the spirit meet and differentiate between them, for us.

Jude

Taking God's Prophets

The Dream:
The roads turned and turned. It was difficult to find my way on this freeway. When I get to the top, still I am not on the road to the church. I look over the edge and it is nearby, but there is not way to get there from here. I must go back and come around the corner to get there. For, I need to pick up my assignment for the day. I am a student and going out on assignment with businesses to learn about them.

Interpretation:
The roads to this business are windy and when I think I have reached the top, I find that they merely look over where I want to be, rather than bringing me there. Big business looks down on the Church, rather than leading to it. The assignment that God has for me is directed from Him rather than big business. He is the top of this business.

The principles of this business are set in stone built from an old plan and given to others with gentleness. This business is about training others in His business.

In the dream I make my way to the church. It is an old building, set in stone. I am greeted by a nice woman who gives me my assignment for the day. I am sure that I must go to a business that is nice, so I look that direction, but it is not to be so. I am called back because this assignment is not mine today. I am sent back to the same place as yesterday.

What I have hoped for is a nice little business similar to a gift shop. I thought that I would be selling information related to the gifts from God in a nice way. Everything was to be bathed in the love of God, immersed in the Holy

Spirit, but that is not the way it has been playing out. As much as I want this assignment, it is not mine, today. I am supposed to go where I am to be trained in business.

I go to the place that looks like a gift shop. I wind my way up some very steep stairs. This one is on Main Street, but has no window to the street. It is upstairs facing toward the backstreet. I don't see how they sell anything from this shop.

But, this is bad business training. It looks like they could train in the gifts of the Holy Spirit, but they don't. They sell them for prophet. They are selling ill feelings and lies. They have made the entrance difficult to get to. Even though they have gifts to sell, they make it so difficult to get to that most can't find the entrance to the store.

In this place there are men squabbling over the sales. The artists are frustrated people who are prejudiced against based on what they produce. People are seeing their art as an extension of them and calling them 'weird'. They are having a problem making a living. I have been sent to a workplace that I think is mine. It was mine yesterday, so I assume it is mine today.

They take credit for everything and expect you to pay for things they don't give you. The true artists are frustrated, being called weird. They are unhappy and poor, being put down by those who manage them. Their art is thrown in a corner, only occasionally pulled out to make a profit for those who wish to elevate their own account. They use others to raise themselves up.

I am sent to a place that I think is mine, because it was yesterday. Yesterday, I was thrown in the corner and used by others to raise their account. They discounted my name and took away my joy. Because I have been down trodden before, I assume I will continue to be.

But, I am met by an angry woman who tells me that

I am ruining her business. She sends me away because she, declares that I have done something wrong. I am not aware of anything that I have done to her, but because she is the owner of this place, I will leave. I was only there for training, anyway. She says that I have done bad yesterday, so she does not want me back today. I am surprised at her attitude, but feel like she is the one controlling her business.

But, I think I have ticked off the management of bad business, somehow without knowing. I am greeted by anger and the assumption that I am ruining her business. If her business is ruined, I am sure it is by herself, not me. She sends me away. She declares that I have caused her problems by something I did yesterday. I wasn't aware then, but I think I know now. For, I have declared that the door is open for God's business. In declaring His truth to be open, I am sure that hers is closed. She will be run out of town. And, I have the nerve to step into her office! Certainly she knows that I am the one who has declared open house on truth, for now she will be closed down. Who will come for the lies when the truth is available? Am I surprised at her attitude? I shouldn't be. The enemy will be angered at me when He learns that I am promoting the truth about the voice of God and hearing Him in dreams. They will be upset because I will ruin their profits, and their image. But, the truth is that they don't have a nice image to start with. They have always been liars, only now someone has declared it openly. When I came to train, I was shown the difference. I see their style of business as oppressive, and it's not of the Church. Certainly, this is not authorized by God, but is of another.

That is OK, I will just go back and receive another assignment to a different office. I didn't choose hers anyway, it was given to me. I certainly don't want to project her image to others. She is rude and selfish. Hers is small and she is mean to her workers, demeaning them personally.

And, do I run my business like hers? Certainly not. My business is not for my own profit, but to train prophets, and promote artists for God. For, certainly we will project the owner of our business, whoever it is. Do we own our own business, or are we owned by another?

Now, I need to return to the Church for another assignment. I am sure they have other places of business that they will send this student to.

As I leave, I go down several levels of stairs. At the landing there is a rack of fabric that has fallen from her place. Even though her presentation is poor, I do not mean her any harm or disrespect and pick up her merchandise from the floor, rather than trampling it underfoot. I only walk away, not wish ill on her and her type of marketing. What I step over is a fallen rack of banners. I pick them up and hang them over the railing. Banners over railing. The mean ugly business manager does not thank my for picking up her fallen banners, but only is concerned over making money. Whether it is a flag or a shirt, I am not sure, still it would be a shame to leave it laying there to be stepped on as I leave. They belong hung, not to be stepped on.

I have something to add to all business, no matter how awful it is. I pick up their banners and hang them on the railing. What that means is that I can see their true purpose, even through the one that they project. I have the ability to see what their intended purpose is. Many put aside their true purpose and seek to make money instead. I have the ability to be sympathetic with them, instead of riling them back.

And, I have a stubborn one on a leash I am trying to pull through. It's like a burro. It's like I need to go through a building and over a rail. Shelly is cheering my on. I try to go back the way I came, but it collapses. The whole thing goes flat, like a tent. Once the roof comes down, I realize that there is no need to walk through because, now I can freely step around the problem. I can by pass the situation.

This is a stubborn situation because most business is run with the intent on making money as their primary purpose. Their purpose is for profit. Mine is for prophet. I am trying to pull through a tough idea. As I go through all of the railing of others, it will soon become apparent that I don't need to go through it. I simply walk around it, I by pass it. It's my flag. Just hang it on the rail.

And, I am going back to the Church and tell them about this bad business because there is deception in there. That woman is a liar and a thief. She doesn't care about anyone, but her selfish self. She is cruel to her workers and sends the students away without training them, finding fault without error.

And, God is sending me back to the Church, the place where I started, to tell them about this bad business where people are making a profit rather than making prophets. For, the prophets are being treated poorly and taken advantage of. They are not for others to profit from, but for the Church to profit from. All the prophets are God's business.

Check-in Closet

Everlasting righteousness is yours eternally
because Jesus bared His soul
to the whole world.
He shared
Himself.
He opened up His walk in closet.
The place where His garment is kept.
He unlocked the door and gave us the key.
Anyone may go to that closet. It's a closet of prayer.
And ask Him for something to wear. It's like an eternal
coat closet
when you pick up your coat after a party. We can pick up
our coat from the team
at the door.
The only difference is we never checked a coat in.
We don't bring one with us. He just provides.
Righteousness freely given to us
one by one
when we go to
the check in closet.

God's Presence

God's presence is a state of being that surrounds us. He is sovereign, yet He makes a personal appearance with His invisible Spirit. He is felt and seen with our spirit.

When did we stop believing that God is everywhere? He is. There is nowhere we can run from His presence. If we are doing bad things this could be a problem.

I have wondered how Satan came into the presence of God in the book of Job. Well, if God's presence is everywhere, then all Satan had to do is stand still and he was in the presence of God.

The difference there was that God showed Himself to Satan and spoke to him. It was up to God whether or not to talk to Satan.

Hopefully, we do not fear the presence of God, but delight that He is near to us. He was there when we were formed in the womb. His eye has always been on us. He had plans for us then. He wants to hem us in with His presence. We should feel him so close to us that He encircles everything we do.

If his presence is always there, why don't we sense it?

When Jesus ascended into heaven, He gave us the Holy Spirit, His presence, that we might always have Him nearby.

He says that He has not left us as orphans, but why do we sometimes feel abandoned? We are the ones holding back on the relationship. God does not take authority over our meetings that we have with Him, unless we invite Him.

Often, we do not want God to direct our encounters, so we hide from Him. It is not like we need to go under a rock to hide from Him.

No. All we need to do is not invite Him. Then He will not come. He does not come where He is not wanted.

He comes to us His way. If we do not invite Him His way on His terms, He will not come. He does not need us. He is God. He desires our presence. But, remember, He has already done all He can to make Himself available to us.

It was the blood of his Son that broke down the dividing wall between us and Him so that we could live in His presence. Jesus Christ become for us what it takes to get us to that place.

When Jesus presents us to the Father, He doesn't point out our sins, but that He has paid the price for them; they are covered under His blood.

He has opened a way to the Father's presence for us.

Therefore, we are able to draw near to God with a sincere heart in full assurance of faith, having our hearts sprinkled to cleanse from a guilty conscience.

When we give our hearts to Jesus, the Holy Spirit dwells in us. His presence within us, gives us ability to become obedient to God's ideals.

When we permit the program that He has laid out to flow in and through us, we will experience the presence of God. We will feel it move. It flows.

The presence of God needs to move through the gifting that He has given us. He has not put us in a position, then walked away. He is not idle

We are not like eggs waiting to be hatched at the end of the age. He wants us to be active for His purposes.

Only when the Holy Spirit flows through us, can we have a ministry. The Lord has thousands of ways He wants to use to display Himself to the world. These are the gifts that He has given to us as we move closer into His realm. When we dwell in Him and He dwells in us, then His love will start to overflow onto others.

His voice to us will bring the training that we need to do the job that He calls us to do. Our relationship with Him needs to be in motion, as He is in motion. It is as if the Kingdom of God is a train passing by. We need to continue to look out the window seeking direction from God if we want to be used by Him.

When we take breaks in our relationship with Him, then it is as if we are looking inside the train and will miss the scenery. We won't know where we are in relationship to other things within the Kingdom of God.

Gen 3.8, Ex 33.14, Lev 22.3, Job 1.12, Ps 16.11, 31.20, 68.2, 95.2, 114.7, 139, Isa 64.1, Heb 9.24, I co 1.29, Jude 24, John 14.15-26.

Famine of the Words of God

Prophecy has entered the bedroom:
I have removed the door.

Foretelling and forth telling the Word of God providing direction and encouragement to His people has entered where the Church sleeps. Prophecy has come to awaken it. To remove the door, it must be taken off the hinges. God is using us as tools, not just to open the door, but to remove it forever.

The Dream

I am in a mud room of a house (ante-room where you remove your boots before entering the house). The door is open and a large beautiful black bird flies into the room. It is a tropical bird with shiny feathers and a crimson ring around its eye. It talks to me. It has flown in through the garage because the door is open.

I follow the bird out into the garage. It takes the garage door opener and hides it up in the rafters out of my reach. Then, it shows me some caged birds. As I look at the caged birds, I notice two green parrots who have only known captivity and two beautiful blue baby birds who have been caught and put into the cage.

The blue birds are sad and look like they are about to die. They are walking amidst the droppings in the bottom of the cage. As I pick up the cage under the instruction of the black bird, there is no back to the cage at all. Once the cage is picked up, the birds could fly free.

He tells me to let the blue birds go free and to place the parrots in with the puppies who are caged in the garage. There are four puppies, as there were four birds. They are in a cage in the center of the garage. This cage does not have any walls, but the puppies are staying in.

Interpretation:

The black bird symbolizes God's words carried through His messenger service on the wind (the Holy Spirit). It often comes through the darkness in the form of the gift of dreams at night. The red circle around the eye gives special attention to the vision, which is encircled by representation of the blood of Jesus. The blood of Jesus Christ encircles the vision of the words for His people.

The messenger finds me in the ante-room with my shoes removed as I realize that going into the dwelling place of God (the presence of His Holiness) requires cleansing. The bird is a tame bird that has been taught to say only what the master wants it to say. God's vision for us is to be totally free as He takes the garage door opener and moves it out of the way. A garage is a place where things are stored for the 'next season'. As God has taken me to the garage, He makes me aware that the 'tools of God' need to be taken out at their seasons. We have stored them rather than listen and be aware of when God wants to use His tools in His Kingdom. He longs to build a Kingdom. The caged birds are innocent truths that God has provided for His people. Rather than building a nest for them, they have put them in storage. The cage is of deception built by the enemy. Thinking we need to 'save things for a different season'.

The cage is a weaving of deceit by the enemy to which we are being held in captivity. Waywardness and complacency caused by our stubbornness and rebellious heart have caused us to turn from having God being in charge of our lives. We have permitted our Church to be taken captive by Satan. We have listened to false prophecy because it has allowed us to be complacent.

We haven't given to the true needs of the people. We

have taught them to be religious. The true needs are companionship with God and nurturing by the Divine Shepherd.

We need to release prayer and praise within the Church. The birds are representative of prayer...the ones on the floor that are blue...and praise...the parrots that sing all the time, even when caged. There are two of each because they are called to reproduce. God is always interested in having spiritual children.

The puppies represent companionship with the master. We need to take them out of storage and bring it into the bedroom. The bird tells me to allow the parrots to join the puppies and to release the blue birds. Prayer would be released, and praise would become joined with companionship with Our Shepherd. All need to be taken out of the garage because it is the season.

The promises of God have been paraphrased by those put in charge of the house. There is a deceit of humanism and flesh. They are for self-gain and spend more time placating each other than caring for the needs of the people. They have caged the birds and the puppies. They have put them into storage, and are killing them. They have thrown prayer, praise and intimacy with the master out of the house. They do not clean the cages, even.

The teachings are not pure, but have their own sweepings mixed in. There are those who sicken, rather than release the newborns. There are those who do not preach from a pure heart, yet, expect loyalty and following. They sell the sweepings with the wheat. Gossip and smut with the words of the Lord.

The word of God is no longer coming in through the front door, He has removed the garage door by opening it permanently. He will swoop in with dreams of the night and speak to His people, Himself. It has become a door that cannot be closed. His desire is for this to be a season of praise, intimacy and prophecy brought into the Church through cleansing. To enter the house in the dream, one must go through the ante-room, remove your boots and wash up.

There is a time of purification that is needed for the house and, it's coming in through the back door. There has been a famine of hearing the words of the Lord, but now is the season to remove the tools that we have put into storage and learn to listen to His voice.

Psalms 104, Proverbs 1, 6.1-5, 26.2, Ecclesiastes 12.1-14, Isaiah 31.5, Jeremiah 12, Lamentations 2, Hosea 11, Amos, Matthew 8.20, 13, Luke 9.58, Romans 1.18, Revelation 18.

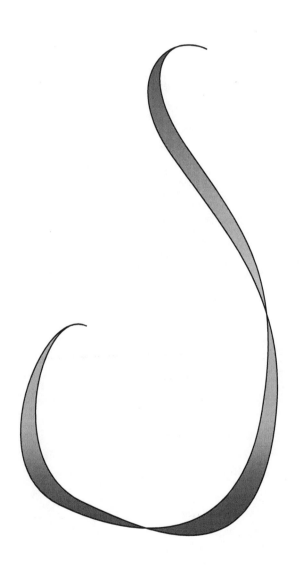

Section 4

Practicing Prophetic Prayer

Hearing from God
Visions, dreams, art, and nature

    A vision is a " Mental representation of external objects, or scenes. An object that comes up in the mind." (Funk & Wagnalls Dictionary).
    In order for an artist to paint a picture, he must first have a mental representation of it . It has to be built in his mind. He has to visualize it, dream it. Then, in obedience to the vision, he puts it into action and builds it, "just like he saw it". In essence, artists have visions that are transferred to canvas. The impressions are first 'etched' on their mind, then transferred to the paper for others to see. They try to make it 'just like they saw it.'
    There are over one hundred references to dreams and visions in the Bible. Many individuals had visions. In Acts 10, Cornelius has a vision in which God tells him to accept Paul and pray over him to receive his sight again. Each of the book of Prophecy in the Scriptures are visions that have been transferred to paper by the author when God 'etched' it on their mind. Jeremiah, Ezekiel, and Revelation all are written in symbolic form. They could be 'painted'. They are all visionary and prophetic. Often

God speaks to us in an unconventional manner. We need to be open to listen to Him.. We do not limit God when we don't listen to Him, we limit His work in our lives

We are not to ignore the dreams and visions, but to become faithful to speak their meaning faithfully according to God's intention of the message. The visions are to have a firm foundation in the Scriptures. As we trust God for the foundation of each vision, He is faithful. Visions bring a God that is active into our lives showing direction for our prayers. {He who has a dream let him tell it, He who has my word speak it faithfully. What does straw have to do with wheat? Is not my word a fire and a hammer that breaks the rock into pieces? Jer 23:28-30.}

When we come to know Jesus Christ intimately, we will learn to recognize his signature on the artwork. All artists sign their artwork. You can tell who painted a piece of artwork if you know the artist's work. We need to come to know God intimately so we can recognize the dreams, visions and revelations that are from him.

There are those with a special gift of prophecy who have a close relationship with God. He has taught them to listen well, and tell the desires of his heart to others. They know his character because they have spent time getting to know him. They know that God signs His art work. The deeper level of prophecy is associated with intimacy with Jesus Christ through the Holy Spirit. Paul, in the New Testament, said it was a desire of his heart that all would become prophets to this level. God desires us all to recognize His signature. He is doing a lot of art work that we are not crediting Him for.

Historically, God has spoken to his people through Prophets. A prophet was an individual who became the 'mouthpiece' of God. The Lord would put words into their mouth and send them to speak to groups of people to get them to follow His ways. These individuals were consecrated (set apart) and anointed (given special ability) to do whatever mission God wanted them to do. Moses, Aaron, Jeremiah, Isaiah, John the Baptist were prophets.

Visions and dreams throughout the Bible provide direction: Daniel 2:3 Nebuchadnezzar had a dream. His spirit became " anxious to understand the dream." He knew that he must interpret the dream because it was telling him how to run the kingdom. The dream ended up being interpreted by Daniel. It provided information needed to warn about a famine that was to come onto the land.

Prophetic Dreams
How to Interpret Dreams

Message of the Dream

The message of the dream should move us closer to God because that is the goal of God in all of His interactions with us. The dream might reveal areas of sin. If we have been praying for God to reveal some hidden sin in our life, perhaps He will give us a dream (Ps 51). Maybe there needs to be a change in our life. Perhaps we are off the track that God wants us to be on. He will, often, reveal this to people in dreams. If we are in a position of authority, God, often will speak to us about individuals whom are under our authority. This will provide direction what to do with them to help them to move closer to Him.

Another area where God talks to individuals through dreams is with "Strongholds". Strongholds are areas in our lives of bad teaching where have learned something wrongly, and God is trying to tell us to relearn it His way.

Dreams may be prophetic; insight to provide direction to decisions for the future. They also provide heart direction, if your heart needs to be realigned to God. The direction may be immediate, or lifelong.

Remember that dreams are like boxes to be delivered to our doorstep. They have stickers on the other side of the box.

This means that if we have had a dream several years ago, there is another message, if we ask God to turn it over again.

We can revisit each dream time and time again. A dream may be timely with a message, but it also has a bigger message for another time. Only a message from God could do that!

How to come up with God's Message:

It is important to not try to interpret the dream from any other source than the Bible and God Himself. I do not interpret other's dreams. I can't. No one can. I can, however, ask questions, that if the individual answers, will lead to the meaning of the dream.

I will show you:

First, write down the dream. A dream is like a piece of art. If you stand too close, then you can't see the whole picture. If you have an empty note book nearby the bed at night, then you will be more likely to write them down. Jesus said that if we are faithful in a little, then He will give more. If He gives you dreams and you do not write them down, then why would He give more?

One of the reasons, I am sure, that I have so many dreams, is that I have made an effort to write them down and find out their meanings. I have many dreams, however, that I have not written down and still more that I wrote down, but have never figured out. Dreams are mysteries that need to be unraveled by the Word of God and the presence of the Holy Spirit.

After you write down the dream, step back. Often times, He plays on words. Sea doesn't mean the ocean, but see. A father in a dream can mean your real father or the Father in Heaven. A sister could mean your sister in the flesh, or it could mean your brethren at church. I use a dictionary to help me expand my thinking. I write each word on a piece of paper and try to think of as many meanings as possible for the words. A locked door in your dream may cause you to think about an entrance in your life that is 'locked'. Dreams are metaphorical.

You need to expand your mind. It is a matter of starting to think outside of your box. It is the beginning to learning to think using the mind of Christ.

Next, ask God about the true message of the dream. He will guide and help if you ask Him. Take the written details of the dream and look up the words in the Bible

Some of the weirdest dreams have become the most profound, for me, when I took them back to Him. The first time I had a naked dream, I was worried that Satan had entered my dreams. So I asked. What He said is that my nakedness within the dream simply shows that I am willing to be open with Him. I am naked, just like when I was born. It is not a bad thing to God.

Allow Him to give the meaning to the dream apart from human language. For example, In the Bible, Jesus is called a door, and individuals go 'through' Him.. Try to take the language out of the symbols of the dream and allow them to be interpreted by God's viewpoint. Many Bibles have cross references to verses that can add understanding to passages. Read these for additional insight into meanings.

A concordance is helpful. It is a book, similar to a dictionary, which has words listed in the Bible. It is usually found in the back of a Bible and the words are listed alphabetically. It gives a reference in the Bible where a verse can be found with that word in it.

Sit quietly and ask questions to God. Have paper and pen ready to copy His answers. I take my dreams to the desert hiking with me and talk to God. I ask Him questions and copy the answers. I used to take an index card. Now I take a notebook.

Once, when I had a dream that I could not figure out, God intervened in a special way. There were crabs in the dream. I don't care how much you tear the Bible apart; there are no crabs in it. So, I was perplexed about what those were. I had pretty much constrained myself to thinking that they were evil things lurking in dark places eating trash.

Two weeks after I had the dream I was met by a friend in the hall. She was a work acquaintance who I did not really know. But, she stopped me dead in the hall and said, "Sheri, I had a dream last night. You and I were at bar eating crabs all night."

Well, I was even more stumped. To think I was eating these evil things lurking!

So, I went back to God and the Bible with the new piece that she provided. It led me to the answer of the dream. The crabs did represent sin.

So, went to the woman who had the dream and I confessed to her that her dream had interpreted mine. So, I asked her if she would like my dream to be used to interpret hers.

She came to my house and I did both dreams side by side. They formed a beautiful picture of how Jesus provides forgiveness for our sins. Her side of the dream related to how He forgives us once and for all. Mine was on how He forgives all other sins on a continuing basis.

She prayed with me and turned her life over to God at my kitchen table that morning at seven AM over a box of donuts. Don't underestimate the power of dreams.

What is Prophetic Art?

When we pray, God answers us. When He does, often, we don't recognize it because it isn't in a form that we are looking for. We don't see the art as messages from God because we don't fathom His Love for us His constant desire to be in our life. He comes into our world in unusual ways. We were created by God in the beginning to keep Him company. (Gen 3:8). In the beginning Adam and Eve walked side by side with God. God desires communication with us. He has sought us from the time He created us. We turn away from him. We lost our relationship with Him when Adam and Eve sinned in the Garden of Eden (Gen 3:34). Every since then He has been working on a plan to get us back into HIs presence.

He speaks, but often we do not recognize him because we don't recognize his voice. (John 10:4) And if we don't recognize his voice, how will we know which way to go? Following the voice of God will provide direction to our lives.

This is how I see God trying to talk to us: He is big, after all he created the whole world including all the galaxies. Let's suppose he wants to get a message to us. Pretend you are big and have a family of ants that you want to get a message to. They would not understand the things in your 'big' world because they only see things from their perspective in the grass. They don't speak English and you do not speak 'ant language' so the only means of communication you could use is to select things from their environment as teaching tools and demonstrate what you want to teach them. In a similar manner, God doesn't speak 'English' because he is God and we are not. He is so far above us that we can not understand him either. But because he desires to get his messages across, he picks things that we can relate to in our little scope of the world and demonstrates teaching principles. He gives us visions and we must bring them into our consciousness and transfer them onto a medium that can be visualized with our eyes before we can understand what he wants to teach us.

He uses the things in creation and puts them onto the canvas of our minds. The gifts he has instilled in us transfer them to the canvas. He uses the canvas of our minds to draw his pictures. A picture has to be visualized by an artist before it can be painted. When an artist has this 'vision' burned on his mind, he cannot rest until it is let out by what ever medium he uses to display his ideas. God delivers his messages through assigning individuals to specific duties in the Kingdom of God.

Why does He give us the Message?

Our primary purpose is to utilize our talents to praise Him. We have been entrusted with gifts which we are supposed to develop for the use of the Church body. When we become complacent in the use of them, there is a curse of God that will bring withered hands and blindness. Obedience to use the gifts God has entrusted us with allows us to become slaves to righteousness which leads to Holiness. Sharing our gifts with others brings unification of the body of Christ and permits others to enter into our acceptable sacrifice of Praise.

Many times others do not see our 'talent'. We may

become discouraged. But , we must remember that we are living in a time that the enemy is fighting hard against us. He knows that he has only a short time and he will be chained in Hell forever. Even though, as loyal servants of Christ, we are spread out, do not be discouraged. He has called us and He will multiply us because of His righteousness. We are supposed to bring everything into the house of God, so the temple can be built. God needs every tool for the Kingdom of God to be built. Just because others may say that your art is bad, in God's eyes it is an essential tool that he needs to display his character and teaching. We are the display of God's righteousness to the world through our gifts in unity with our relationship in Christ Jesus. As children of God, he calls us stars in his Kingdom. He wants us to shine for Him. Just like comets, we are in motion and each display a tail of a different color. No two stars are alike. We all shine for him, but display different characteristics within his Kingdom. There may be many with similar gifts, but each has a wonderful tail of a different color.

Visions

A vision is a mental representation of something that is not tangent. You can't reach out and touch it. Often, when we pray for another person, we may have a symbolic vision that comes up into our mind. It may be a scene, or a thing, or a person (rarely). There are many individuals in Holy Books that had visions or trance states.

In Acts 10 (Christian New Testament) Cornelius has a vision in which God tells him to accept Paul and pray over him to receive his sight again. Each of the books of Prophecy in the scriptures are either visions or dreams. Jeremiah, Ezekiel, (Old Testament) and Revelation (New Testament) all are written like someone who is on drugs. They are all visionary and prophetic. Often, God speaks to us in an unconventional manner. We need to be open to listen to Him. *God is not limited by our refusal to accept the visions and pray into them, we only limit our access to information that will help us with the answer.* He will only use willing vessels. Visions can give direction to prayer.

The English Interpretation of the Qur'aan (by Abdullah Usuf Ali) has much to say regarding visions, inspirations and dreams. In Surah 20 the vision of Moses with the burning bush is reviewed for all to remember that Moses was walking and talking when this vision came to him so real that it caused him to eventually lead a people out of Egypt.

In Surah 40.15 it says, "Raised high above ranks (or degrees), (He is) the Lord of the Throne (of authority): by His Command He sends the spirit (of inspiration) to any of His servants He pleases, that it may warn (men) of the day of Mutual Meeting."

Indeed, The Lord gives guidance to His servants when they seek Him in reverence and desiring mercy with His grace which is freely given.

Surah 34.50 of the Qur'aan says that "If I am astray, I only stray to the loss of my own soul: but if I receive guidance, it is because of the inspiration of my Lord to me: it is He Who hears all things, and is (ever) near."

Oh, how we thank Him that He is ever near, and we lift our praise to Him for the inspiration which He freely gives when we seek Him with a pure heart.

The Old Testament full of dreams and visions which were given to the Prophets to give them guidance.

Beginning with Genesis 15.1 God made His covenant with Abram using a vision. He declares all that will be given to him as if a man was speaking to a man face to face. It seems to be different from the Angel who spoke to Hagar in the desert after she had fled from Sarai. An angel speaking to someone is a spiritual being, not a vision of something. It is really there. A vision is a picture of something (present, past or to come). In this way a vision is just like a dream, except the individual is awake and not sleeping. Sometimes people are asleep, then the vision continues to move into the day time as it the dream continues.

I have only had this happen to me once: And that is when I wrote down Vacuum Cleaner Salesman as a piece and compiled it with two other writings to make Abreas Ansus. I was asleep having the dream and woke up. I went to the computer to put the dream into the computer (this was about 5 A.M.). It's just that the dream kept coming and I knew that I could type it faster than I could write it down.

So, I wrote it down as I walked into it. In essence, it was me that went door to door seeking someone who would 'buy' what I had to sell. I needed my prayers answered: I needed someone to buy 'my story'. There was a tremendous amount of passion and pain that I felt as the vision kept coming to me. The tears tore down my face as I struggled to see what I was putting onto the paper. Only by inspiration could this come to my, I am sure of that, for the whole thing remains exactly as I wrote it down that morning in 45 minutes. I typed it in then went back and formatted the goblet shapes in about 15 minutes. Then, I took a shower and went to work. You see, I have to leave for work at 6:30, so I know exactly how quickly the vision came to me.

Let me encourage you to write down your visions. And, try to grab as many threads from heaven as you can whether they come as dreams or words into your spirit. Then, take the vision and interpret it using Scriptures as an outline for criteria. Many of my books have visions in them which I interpret, so you can see how I do it using Scriptures which are familiar to you. Then, ask the Lord to send you His Spirit of Truth into your soul to give you understanding of the answer. He will because the only reason He gives a vision is to give you direction, so I am sure that He wants you to have it. Think about someone asking for a map to get some where and a neighbor over hears that he needs a map, so he tosses it over the fence in the back yard. Don't you think he sent it over the fence for a reason? Of course. He wants to help the one on the other side.

We are like the one on the other side of the fence and the Lord has provided a means to send a map on over the fence for us. You see the thing with a map is that it does no good to have a map if you don't know where you are on it. Like one of those mall maps, we need a blue star to show us where we are starting out from so we can see where we need to go to get to where we need to be.

The vision is like the blue star on the mall map. If we can figure out the vision (or dream or words from heaven) then we will become oriented to where we are in relation to the way God sees things (that's the map). It is the Spirit that knows the mind of God, so certainly He knows how He thinks about where we are in life and where we need to be. So, when we combine the guidance of the Spirit with the vision, we will have greater understanding from the vantage point of the one who sent the message in the first place.

Let us beware, however, that there are not from God. Many see visions when they are on drugs, coming out of anesthesia and withdrawals from alcohol. (I know because I am an Nurse.) Also, Satan is called the 'Great Impersonator', so it makes sense that he could send a vision to lead someone the wrong way. Do not allow your fear of this keep you from pressing forward to understanding your visions. What if they are a message from God and you have been ignoring them all along? Do you want to face God, in the future having torn up the mail He has attempted to deliver to you to help guide you along life's paths?

The way to tell the difference is easy. Jesus said that you can tell a tree by it's fruit. A good tree bears fruits of righteousness. When you attempt to understand the vision, if it from Heaven, it will yield the fruits of righteous living. Certainly you would not follow a vision to harm your brother or wound your children! These are not visions which yield fruits of righteousness.

I have the many pages of this 'Vision Journal' blank for you to write down your visions because I am certain, that If you seek the vision; look toward wanting to know where you are on the map in relation to where God wants you to be, then He will give you visions, dreams and inspirations from heaven.

And, when you have the vision, seek to understand it. Correlate it with Scriptures, ask the Spirit of Truth to help you with Divine Inspiration, and walk toward the answer. Why else would you have a map in your hand, but to walk in the direction in which you need to go.

References:

Old Testament: *Numbers 12.6, Ezekiel 1.1, Proverbs 29.18, Daniel 1.17, Hosea 12.10, Habakkuk 2.3, Job 33.15, Isaiah 22.1*
Book of Mormon: *Lehi overcome by a vision I Nephi 1.7,8, Alma 8.20*
New Testament: *2 Corinthians 12.1, Acts 2.17, Acts 10.3, Revelation 9.17*

Speaking in Tongues

What is speaking in tongues?
Tongues is a spirit voice. It comes to when those who receive the Baptism of the Holy Spirit open themselves to receive it. The Baptism of the Holy Spirit frees the individual's spirit to commune with God's Spirit and there is a joining of spirits. When he asks for this gift, then opens His heart to receive it, then the breath of God is put behind his. The Holy Spirit is called the 'breath of God'. When someone receives the breath of God, then, he is able to open up a different avenue than he had before.

The breath of God becomes the air behind a voice that hasn't been heard before. The person speaks a new voice; the voice of the Holy Spirit. We can move our mouth, but without breath, others can't hear us. The Spirit provides the breath, giving the words a sound. Those that receive the Baptism of the Holy Spirit simply open themselves up to be used by God to allow His breath to pass through them. (See Holy Hum)

Why do they do it?
Many speak in tongues because it gives a rush. Having the Spirit of God use their voice to speak is so weird, that they look for it. Like a junkie looking for a fix, they want the rush of the power of God flowing from their insides out.

Others just want to get close to God and know that when they open their way to His, it forms a special bond between them. It gives them confirmation that they have the Holy Spirit living inside, for they certainly could not make up a voice that they never learned.

Still, others use tongues to speak back to God, because they believe that it is a prayer 'tongue' that is like He is present. When they pray 'in tongues' it is as if they can form perfect prayers that will certainly be answered because they are from God and if the prayers originate from God, then He will answer them. (See Tómaseña)

It looks fake, how can I tell the difference?
Some speak in tongues and it is fake. Satan is a master of deception, so why wouldn't he fake tongues coming out of someone. Others speak in tongues because they are trying to impress those around them, but just like other things, we can ask God to show us the difference.

God doesn't like fakes; especially someone faking something that is supposed to be from Him, so ask Him if it's for real. He will tell you.

Another way you can tell the difference is if someone has the gift of Interpretation of Tongues. With this gift, the individual is able to tell what the words say. Because it is a gift from God, then when the interpretation is given, the power of God falls and all who are in the room feel it. I know, because I have it. Like tongues, it is a gift that God gives when we ask for it. (See Camezía Reptídad)

Speaking in Tongues and Prayer

There are three types of tongues gifts

1. Tongues as evidence of Holy Spirit's filling. It is a human language supernaturally coming forth, so that all the people will know that it is the Spirit. This is profound because we realize that God is speaking. No man understands it. It is not an old language, but language that is to be interpreted. God's word flows through. They are to revive the people; they are to give new depths of thought (Ephesians 3). It is like the man inside closing down and the Holy Spirit taking over (Wigglesworth 171).

2. Prayer tongues: direct language to God in prayer. Sometimes you can be so full of the Holy Spirit that the joy of my body is more full than my language can express. Then, instantly, the Spirit pours forth His word in tongues, and the power of God just lifts the whole place into revelation and words of life far beyond where we were (P174 Wiggles).

3. Revelation and power to the Church to lift the saints and fill the place with God's Glory. It has to have interpretation because God is speaking to us in words that are not in our native language Tongues bring forth revelation and power in the Church, to save it from lack and from being bound. Tongues and interpretation are for liberty among the people, to lift the saints and fill the place with Glory. These people are so moved by the Spirit that they are in a place where they know that what God was burning within had to come out. No interpreter has the interpretation, not one. They have the spirit of it, and they knew it was according to the mind of God. They got the

sense of the knowledge that God was speaking and that it was the Spirit, and they knew it was right. The Spirit breathes the whole thing, and the interpreter speaks as the Spirit gives utterance. So it is as divine and as original as the throne of God. (Wigglesworth).

Speaking in tongues with interpretation of tongues for prayers is a powerful directional tool that God gives. When we speak in tongues, it is the mind of God. It is his will for the situation. If we have the ability to interpret the tongues so that we can understand it, we can further add scriptures to it to build a picture of what God wants. If we build the picture and walk into it by prayer, we are walking by faith.

Interpretation of Tongues

There is a gift of tongues and the gift of interpretation of tongues. Many of the words written in these books comes from interpretation of tongues. The titles are tongues. I have interpreted them. With interpretation of tongues, when the language in interpreted, all know it is true because their spirit bares witness with the Spirit of God that these are words from Him. It does not require additional explanation. When I pray over people, many times I speak in tongues very slowly, one word at a time, and interpret each word. It has tremendous power.

Tongues is a gift from God included in the list of spiritual gifts (I Corinthians). It comes to someone who asks for it after he has received the baptism of the Holy Spirit. It is one of the evidences of the Holy Spirit. A language is given that flows out as we make our self available to Him. We provide the air and the willingness. That is all. He provides the subject, and the direction of the talk. We can choose to be part of it, or not.

I have chosen to become part of the conversation between my spirit and God's Holy Spirit. By asking for the gift of interpretation and allowing it to grow to maturity, we can learn about what His intended purpose is for a situation.

The gift of interpretation is an advanced gift, I believe. It is a combination of faith in believing what your spirit is telling you, is true; and openness to God and others.

Interpreting tongues is similar to interpreting other languages. It is the word of God, so the more of the Bible that we know, the more precise the interpretation is. I have found that many times, the interpretation can be found in the scriptures. God is merely directing us to pray in a specific section of scripture. It is like if you want to have a Spanish interpreter, it is best to find some one that knows a lot of English and Spanish. That individual needs to be familiar with both languages. For me, because I speak English, I need the tongues interpreted in this language. I must know both languages; the spirit language and the English language.

When the foreign tongue comes to someone who intends to interpret, it flows from the Spirit of God to the spirit of the individual and out their mouth. To be able to interpret, because the tongues is an unused language, then the one who interprets, needs to ask God for the answer. So, for me, when someone talks in tongues, I ask God. Then, he tells me the answer. It takes some processing time, because the language has to flow from the other person, to my spirit, then my spirit asks God, He responds, and the answer needs to flow out my mouth in English. What it requires is openness. There cannot be any blocks between my spirit and God, or my spirit and the spirit of the other person. Then, it takes faith to believe that what God is telling you is true. I have to be willing to step out by faith and believe that I am listening well enough to tell someone else what I think He said.

For me, if individuals talk too fast, I can't get it. But, if they slow down and give me some time to process, I can ask God and He will give the answer.

This gift is one of the most exciting gifts of the Holy Spirit. For me, I can ask God questions, and He gives me the answers. I speak in tongues, then interpret and 'walla' out comes the answer. Interpretation of tongues has to bypass the mind because it is not needed to interpret the things of God. Sometimes, I come out with things that don't make sense to me, but make a lot of sense to the individual.

When my daughter first received the gift of tongues,

she kept repeating the same phrase over and over. So, she came to me and asked me what it said. The interpretation was something like, "Thankfulness comes from a spirit willing to be thankful."

I told her that I felt that God wanted her to say 'thank you' to Him for receiving the gift before going on.

She accepted this answer and went her way. She returned a few minutes and said that, indeed, that was her problem.

My other daughter has the gift of interpretation of tongues, as well, but she has not memorized a lot of scripture, as myself. When the interpretation comes to her, she receives the 'essence' of what God is saying. It works for her. I think that the one with interpretation of tongues will have a more precise interpretation if he knows more scripture because God has a tendency to repeat Himself with certain phrases.

Someone will be able to receive the gift of interpretation if he can work on two channels. For me, when someone talks, I listen to God and I listen to the person at the same time. There is an aspect where we need to get our own needs out of the way. We must lay down ourselves in order to have the power flow through. This is a gift that enacts the spirit of Might.

Tongues are a sign for unbelievers. I have had several individuals step closer to God after my praying over them and interpreting the words that I spoke in tongues. It is profound, because they see that you are speaking a language you never learned. Then, they see, next that you know information that is provided by God, because there is no other way it could have come to you. As a sign they give direction for our path.

They also provide adoration to God. He gets all the glory when we speak in tongues, because we step aside.

Discerning Voices

So, the question is how do you know weather the voice you are hearing is from God or the Devil? Jesus said that His sheep know His voice and He calls them each by their name.

Do you know your mother's voice? Does she know yours? But, let us suppose someone could disguise their voice to sound just like your mother. Would you know it was not your mother? Of course. Perhaps, at first, you might be fooled. But, you know your mother. And, you would expect her to talk of things you both know; Things you have both previously talked about.

For, the relationships with people that we are close to, are sort of, like ongoing conversations. We know the topics of interest in the other person's life and Each time we speak to him, we pick up from where we left off the last time we spoke. It is like letters sent.

When my husband was in the military, years ago, the only means of communication was letters. There was no phone conversation because cell phones did not exist and a long distance conversation from a foreign country was too expensive.

It could cost as much as 200 dollars for one chat. So, we sent volumes of letters for a few cents each. The mail was sporadic. It came in clumps as the ship would come into a port or send an Air transport vessel off the bow. So, the letters were all mixed up. It was a real problem. The only way we could continue a conversation, a relationship, was to number the letters. Then, when we received them, the first order of priority was to put them in order. For, only by putting them in order, could the thoughts of the conversation be followed over a long period of time. The individual, could, then plug in their responses, and a very slow conversation commenced. Our relationship with those we are close to is similar. Each time we speak, we ask to open up the next numbered letter. And, because we have sent and received a lot of letters previously, we both know which numbers we are on. So, consequently, if someone disguised herself to sound like your mother, Yet could not follow the interactive volley based on a previous relationship, then, you would know it was not your mother. The same it true with God. If we have an on going relationship with Him we will recognize it is Him when He calls. And, when He talks, He will simply continue with the conversation you have both had recently. It's easy.

You know His voice because He is your father.

Father, I pray we may know your voice, your character, your tones. And, Father, my prayer is that you know mine. Help me to be a person of prayer; interactive prayer. Please take away any fear of hearing Your voice.
Amen

CAFËA

The Way I do it

Cafëa is an acronym which was given to me in a dream. After this was given to me, I began putting the section in the back of my books. Sometimes we learn best, not with a class full of instruction, but by sitting down next to someone and watching her do it. So, the cafëa a section on 'how I do it, or how I did it'. I give no teaching in this section. It is purely testimony.

Capitulate: Surrender to His ways and summarize subject.
Associate: Connect with Him having subordinate status.
Facilitate: Make it easy and convenient. Ask and write it down.
Emulate: Compete for the answer. Vie for the truth against all else.
Appreciate: Become fully aware of the value; to be sensitive to and show gratitude for with an increase in proportionate value to that which is revealed. It's OK to say, "Thanks."

Dedication of a Day

Father, I dedicate this day to You.
Make me new.
I don't like who I was yesterday.
It's not that I was bad.
It's just that I know I wasn't as good as I need to be.
So, Dear Lord, create Your newness within me.
Revive my soul, refresh my spirit.
Light the lamp of the knowledge of You within my heart.
I let go of my way.

I release my fingers of what I cling to and ask for You to put them into your will for me.

Give me grace for the time when I feel that emptiness while my fingers are open from letting go and when You fill me with what I need.

Bridge my uneasiness with the gift of faith, I pray, dear Lord.

Faith to believe You for your promises.
For, in thee, do I put my trust. I love You.

* *

I try to pray this prayer nearly every day of my life because God has the ability to make me new. I believe in a creative type of God. I think He isn't into fixing stuff, but making it new. He isn't into repairing what I have tried to do; but rather setting everything apart for His purposes. If you take apart the prayer above you can see several elements are foundational for prophetic prayer.

I begin by rededicating my self to God. Then I confess I am imperfect and need a Savior to rescue me from my ways. I ask for revival in my soul. I ask for refreshment in the power of the Holy Spirit. I ask for the gift of knowledge to come to my heart, not my mind. Then I voluntarily release my fingers from what I am holding dear, asking for grace which comes from above. I ask for Him to give me with everything I need to complete everything He needs to happen. That's provision. I ask for the gift of faith to believe in the bridge of what He provides spiritually and physically to meet every need, not only in my life but in the lives of others. Then, I remind God that I am relying on His promises; and I ask continued strength to rely upon them. I finish with confirming my love for Him.

Of Foundational Importance

There is no way to stress enough the importance of the foundation of Prophecy being firm. Your ministry will only be as good as your personal relationship with God. Festevia is a book I wrote on spiritual gifts. It relates spiritual gifting like a tree. We have a tree and the out put of our life is like the branches of a tree. We can only extend good fruit if our tree is healthy, nourished and growing. It all begins with us. Everything we produce is a direct outflow from our personal relationship with God.

A Blank Paper

A blank paper I wish I could be
waiting and ready with an empty me
Nothing on my mind: Content just to wait
Relenting will, refusing to bend fate

A blank paper, I wish I could be
available for a note, ready for a quote
Line upon line antidote.

Yet the paper is all used up
filled to full. The paper cup
overflowing with what I got
Jotted by my friends.
It's a lot.
Scribbles of notes.
Happy quotes
To dos and what not to dos

A blank paper I wish I could be
waiting and ready with an empty me
Nothing on my mind: Content just to wait
Relenting will, refusing to bend fate

My Prophetic Foundation

The cafëa is supposed to be a place where I tell you how I did it. How did I get to where I am?

The bottom of it all is memorization of many Scriptures over a period of years.

I went to Bible College and learned some more.

I went to a Church and attempted to join the prayer team. It was very difficult because they were people in a room praying disjointed from one another. There I was rudely introduced to the gift of tongues. There were people walking in circles and yelling in a foreign language without interpretation. So, at the end of the prayer session, I barely even knew anyone's name, let alone what they were praying about.

I read in the Bible men who had entreated God; Samuel when he was called by God, Elijah when he hid from the woman trying to kill him and King David after he lost his first born son. All of these men seemed to have a few things in common. They talked to God like He was the creator of the universe, yet as an individual who cared for them. They knew Him. They expected Him to talk back. It wasn't a one sided shout, but a quiet entreat followed by silence waiting for Him to speak.

Ah, look at Elijah. He knew God was not found in the lightening and thunder, but when it got quiet.

At that time in my life I was hiking in the desert for exercise and listened to rock music along the way. I traded in the rock music for praise music. I had a list of things I was praying for and, at first would roll out the list at the beginning of the walk and ramble on and on until I returned to my car for the drive home.

But, it came to me that I was being selfish and I wondered if my perspective might change if I thanked God before I launched into my list.

So, I decided to praise and thank God for the first half of my hike and then when I reached the top of the small mountain, I would take out my prayer list and pray over the things for the second half of the hike.

An amazing thing happened. When I began to spend the extended time in Praise and Worship, my prayer list shortened shorter each hike until it went away. I found myself spending the entire time in Praise and Worship as I listened to the CDs along the hike.

And, I wondered, "What if I ask God what the answer is to my prayer and pray in the answer?"

I figured there would be a pretty good success rate. I mean, do you suppose Elijah knew it was going to rain down fire to consume the sacrifice when he was put up against the false prophets of Baal? Of course he did. He knew the outcome before he entered the battle.

How? Because he asked.

And, so the only factor missing was my ability to listen. Indeed, God says He wants to talk to us (in the Bible). He is as a father desiring to know His children.

So, I studied these men of faith and took note of their similarities. Humility, dedication, servitude, knowledge of the Scriptures and love of God. The hinge factor is they all had a relationship with God; they were friends of God.

I wondered, "What does it take to be a friend of God?"

My name isn't Abraham or Moses. I am just a regular

person. Can I still be God's friend?

I found myself at the base of a mountain called 'the Fear of the Lord'.

This is when I wrote Miraculeś. I never understood the fear of the Lord before this time. It doesn't mean you are frightened of the majesty and greatness of almighty God.

It compares more to a love relationship. Have you ever been in a relationship with someone you knew loved you more than you did him or her? As he came closer, he demanded more of your heart and asked for you to open areas of your self to him. You got just so close, then you backed off because the relationship was too much. He wanted soo much more than you did and you were not willing to go there.

This is how it is with the fear of the Lord. He loves us more than we can ever love Him and He wants to open up every aspect of Himself to us and have us open every aspect of ourselves. So, we get only so close, then we draw away...in the fear of the Lord. It is really the fear of intimacy. You can read all about it in Song of Solomon.

God is actually very romantic. He invented romance. Remember, He is the one who made the roses to have fragrance and the sunlight to dance in the clouds.

The foundation of the gift of prophecy is dependent on how close you are willing to get to God and how much you are willing to trust in His words.

You will never be absolutely sure of what you hear, but God is happy to confirm His words. Just ask.

Gold Dust

Salvation wasn't our idea.
Why do we build on our own ideas now?
We defile what is pure with our own dust
because we are made of dust. God has
provided us with access to His Wisdom,
Knowledge, Understanding and Revelation.
He has given us the keys
to the Kingdom.
He gives us
gold
dust
that
can be
made into
whatever
He chooses.
His ideas are
eternal and priceless.
When, we follow His plan for
His ideas, we build into His desire.

Read on

This is book one in a series of books on Prophetic Prayer.

Foundational Prophetic Prayer builds a Scriptural and faith based foundation for what Prophetic Prayer is and should do for us and others.
- Purpose of Prophetic Prayer
- Character of Prophetic Prayer
- Hearing from God in many Ways
- Practicing Prophetic Prayer

Manual of Personal Prophetic Prayer is for individuals who want to learn to pray in the prophetic mode.
- Spiritual Prayer
- Benefits of Prophetic Prayer
- Prophetic Gifts
- Using the Gifts as tools to pray

Leading Prophetic Prayer is a book on prophetic prayer within groups.
- Invitation
- Education
- Position
- Leading
- The Meeting

About the Author

Sheri Hauser is originally from Seattle Washington being raised in a family with three siblings. Both of her brothers have attended seminary and her sister, Karna Peck is a professional artist joining her with many of her books.

At the age of 16 she committed her life to Jesus Christ and began to follow Him wholeheartedly. When she graduated from High School she attended Ecola Hall for extended training in Biblical Studies. Years of Bible Study and memorization are evident within the threads of teaching in her books.

In 2001, she began having dreams with understanding on interpretation of them. The dreams led her to self-publish her first book, coríanta, and then eventually grow a publishing company, Glorybound Publishing. At the release of this book (2015) she has 20 published books on dreams, from dreams and hearing the voice of God as well as several children's books. In the midst of her training to learn the publishing industry, she also developed the Glorybound Lasertrain which is a set of templates for digital publishing. This set includes 20 books.

Made in the USA
Columbia, SC
13 October 2022